Golden Marriage

Golden Marriage

—*a couple's autobiography*—

by

Herb and Margaret Dimock

CeShore

Pittsburgh, PA

ISBN 1-58501-002-2

Trade Paperback
© Copyright 1999 Herb & Margaret Dimock
All rights reserved
First Printing—1999
Library of Congress #98-88778

Request for information should be addressed to:

CeShore
The Sterling Building
440 Friday Road
Department T-101
Pittsburgh, PA 15209

Cover design: Michelle Vennare - CeShore
Typesetting: Drawing Board Studios
CeShore is an imprint of SterlingHouse Publisher, Inc.

Printed in Canada

Dedication

This book is for our Grandchildren

Jennifer
Sarah
Benjamin
Carl
Christina
Richard
Laura
David
Evan
Tyler
Gregory
Ann

Contents

A Playwright's Passion
(1938)

To begin with, I was in love with Elsie. No, not Margaret. Elsie! And I think there was a warning handwriting on the wall. But even if the letters had been blazoned in fire, I wouldn't have seen them. I didn't want to see them. At the start I reveled in what I thought would be the best year of my life. I was eager to suck out the sweetest of the sweets.

It took some doing to show me that 1938 was not my year of destiny at all. My whole world had to be turned upside down. Or perhaps the better way to say it would be when at last I found Margaret, my whole world turned right side up. But then our whole life has been a series of topsy-turvy overturnings.

At the beginning of that year I landed in West Hollywood drawn by my passion to be a playwright. During my senior year at the university in Berkeley, Professor Kurtz had introduced me to the plays of Eugene O'Neill and I converted promptly to the belief that drama was the way to transform the human heart. I had seen enough hell through the early thirties—homelessness, unemployment, hunger—to know that I wanted to give my life to heal the wounds that people suffered and to reform society's fumbling systems.

Unfortunately, I couldn't be single-minded about my drama career because I also had the twin challenge to provide for my aging widowed mother, Martha Yale Dimock, and at the same time to free myself from her dominating influence in my life. She had been both supreme inspiration and driving goad. Her long-standing criticism of her younger son played on the words, "Stick to business." "You are lazy, Bert, just like your father, Herbert Dimock, Senior." I hated that innuendo. I knew it wasn't true. I had plenty of ambition.

Professor Kurtz had given me big praise for the one-act play I wrote—a drama of prison life under the title, "White Fire." With great enthusiasm octogenarian benefactress Miss Alice Hilgard had put me in touch with Leonard Bacon, editor of The Saturday Review. More praise. In San Francisco I discovered the Wayfarers Civic Repertory company, and they had been eager to have my budding theater talents. These were powerful spurs to my dreams.

During the twelve months before our West Hollywood relocation I worked hard to prove Mother wrong about my "laziness." I focused intensely on four tasks, any one of which could have taken all my energies. I held down a money-earning job as stationery warehouseman at the San Francisco News Company. I volunteered to serve clandestinely as union organizer to bring the Company under labor contract. At night and on weekends I crafted a radio drama series about college life. And hardest of all I tried to keep Mother reasonably contented in our cramped basement apartment on Clay Street. The year was 1937.

I pushed even harder. I saved every spare penny so that, as I told Mother, "We can break out of this trap and move to Hollywood. You want to write. I want to write. If 'Let's Go To College' is going to get a place on the networks, Hollywood is the place to be."

Mother did want to write. Some of her poetry was excellent. I'm sure my drive came directly through her genes, as well as my childhood home which was full of books and stories and literature. She gave full loving approval to my extraordinary burst of initiative, and when the year wound down she and I left the city by the Golden Gate, on the thinnest of shoestrings—literally, $100 in savings—and made the leap of faith to West Hollywood where my half-brother Don lived.

In good conscience I cannot say that I felt my script would be a world-changer, only that it was about my own experience at Cal, a starter on the path to powerful influence in the world. I dreamed of winning bigger and bigger spots for my message, so that, at last, I could buy stock in some network and become a policy maker about what to put on the air waves. I was an idealistic dreamer.

It was in the first week after our arrival in the southland that I met Elsie. I needed a haircut, and on a cloudy Monday morning I went hunting for a barbershop. I found that West Hollywood had no focus. The scattered buildings of the commercial district on Santa Monica Boulevard were split apart by the naked rail tracks of the interurban trolley line that ran down the middle. The street had none of the glamor of Sunset Boulevard a half dozen blocks to the north. It exuded the same feeling that haunted me, the feel of being on the way to somewhere else.

Divine providence must have led me to exactly the right place, Frank's Barber Shop, several blocks along the street. Quickly I discovered that Frank was the pipeline for information about who was doing what in the neighborhood. He cued me to the presence of a small community of writers and actors who aspired, as I did, to break into radio or film work.

When at last I stood again on the sidewalk and the barbershop door swung shut, a wonderful excitement grabbed me. In my right hand I clutched a fragment of note paper on which Frank had written the name Elsie and an address, the meeting place of the artists.

What to do? Mother would expect me back, but a new world beckoned. I ran fingers uncertainly over my freshly cropped hair while sparse traffic drifted by on Santa Monica and a pair of the big red trolleys rumbled toward the west. I dug a woolly cap out of the pocket of my gabardine jacket and pulled it over my ears to fend off the chill January wind.

Somehow the wind flushed away my uncertainty. Timidity vanished like water from the overnight rainstorm that poured down the grating by the curb. I stepped across the blacktop and the rail tracks over to the south side and hustled eastward to the second intersection. In my heart I knew a rising confidence, that my passion to become a playwright could at last begin to see results.

I located Elsie's house half a block south of the Santa Monica traffic, a two-story affair, in the same kind of working class neighborhood as brother Don's, with paint peeling from the posts that held up the front porch roof. I had no idea who Elsie was or what her role in the group might be; possibly a matriarchal benefactress who wanted to help young artists along the path— like my Miss Hilgard.

I climbed the stairs and knocked on the door of Apt. C. The girl who opened it shook me to the center of my being.

"Hi." Her voice, sweet and musical, matched the open, inviting smile she lavished on the strange young man at her door.

"Are you...is this...I mean...I'm hunting for Elsie." I felt like an absolute dunce.

"That's me." She had a touch of English accent.

"Well, gee. I mean, Frank said your place is...."

"Come in. Any friend of Frank's is a friend of mine." She took my hand and pulled me into her tiny, cheerful apartment, shining with potted flowers on the window sill.

This was too, too much! She was beautiful and tall, almost as tall as my own six feet. I had never before been close to a super-lovely like this. My adolescent dreams of the ideal glamor girl had orbited around movie stars like Mary Pickford or fairy tale heroines like Ozma of Oz. Elsie blew them completely away. Elsie was real, extremely photogenic. Her long blonde hair, smooth skin, and faintly British aura made her infinitely desirable.

As we sat on her sofa I got myself in hand, as well as a young man can who has just been conquered by love-at-first-sight. She was close to my age.

With easy grace she asked, "Your name is...?"

"Herb." I started over again. "Frank said your place is...where actors meet."

"Every Thursday evening," she said. "Are you new to the neighborhood, Herb?"

"Just came down from San Francisco. I've got a radio script and need actors."

Elsie beamed. "You came to the right place. What's the story?"

"A series about college life, based on my life at Cal."

"Sounds great. Can I see it?"

"I'll bring it over tomorrow." And then, because I simply had to find out everything about her, I reached for the stars. "So what's your racket...I mean, your specialty?"

"Acting."

"Movies?" Surely she would be a starlet with that face and that body.

"Not anymore." Her mood grew heavy with reticence.

"What's the matter?"

"I had several good jobs...." She hesitated again. "I was climbing the ladder, and then I discovered there was a price. Directors wanted me to climb into bed with them before they would give me any good roles."

"Oh! That's lousy!"

"So I'm out. Blacklisted. But I wouldn't go back for a million bucks."

I was ready to offer a comforting hand, but the vibes she radiated spoke loudly: "No touching!" I felt a strange paradox in the touch of her hand that pulled me into her apartment and my touch that now she would in no way accept. Maybe that was how she kept control. I was glad to see her firm moral stance. This dream girl was not only beautiful but good. And then our tentative exploration of each other took a quantum leap.

"Are you interested in meditation?" she asked.

"Definitely."

"Have you heard of Krishnamurti, the Hindu guru?"

My eyes lit up. "He's one of my favorite teachers. Ever since my senior year at Ventura High I've been following him. Mother and I often went up to Ojai to hear him talk under the oaks. He's a great spirit."

"I'd love to hear him sometime," she sighed. "I'm reading his books."

For Elsie it was Krishnamurti who tipped the scales in my favor. She couldn't get enough, and I pulled out all the stops. I told her about Krishnamurti's life-mission, which was to critique institutional religion. The more we talked the more I wondered if this was the ONE with whom I could work to bring blessing to the world.

We shared our fascination with esoteric, mystical Eastern philosophy and wondered together about spiritualism and out-of-body experiences. We played around with astrology. I read her palm, which gave me a successful excuse to touch her hands. Clearly Elsie was attracted to me too, but at present only as a spiritual fellow traveller.

When the clock struck twelve my hostess shifted our talk to practical matters. "Would you like to stay to lunch?"

That jolted me awake from my romantic dream. "Oh, gee! Thanks, but I promised Mother I'd be right back. I've got to go. I'll see you tomorrow." I didn't even linger for the courtesy of describing my family scene to her.

I hit the sidewalk at a trot under compulsion to get back to Mother, and then the madness of my choice made me stumble. What was going on? For the first time in my life I had found one to possess my heart, and I walked out. It was crazy. Checking in with Mother wasn't that important. Why, Elsie could be the one to be my life partner. Jeez!

When I pushed through the door of Don's garden cottage nestled in the rear of the landlord's big house, my anger had simmered down to grim endurance. Mother turned from the kitchen sink to dry her arthritic hands on a towel. Lunch was already on the table. There was big question in her brown eyes and also an aura of hurt. I had seen this dozens of times and had vowed each time never to add any more pain. Mother had been through so much suffering: an abusive father, the death of a college lover, two failed marriages, and the long struggle to earn enough to see her two boys through school.

Normally I would tell Mother everything, but this time was different. I could not speak of my safari to Elsie's. The emotions this girl stirred in me belonged to a totally new world. I shucked off my cap and jacket and turned to the cheese sandwich on my plate. Mother moved to stand beside me in a hovering mode.

"Well," she said as she adjusted her apron flowered with blue forget-me-nots. "What have you been doing?"

"Nothing much."

"What took you so long?"

"Oh, I don't know."

"It didn't take you all morning to get a haircut."

"I've been checking out the neighborhood."

"And how many radio stations did you find in West Hollywood?" There was a note of irony in her voice.

I gulped a mouthful of milk before answering. "I learned from the barber that there's a group of young actors in the neighborhood. He says they're hot for any break they can get."

"Did you search them out?"

"They meet Thursday night. That will be my best chance to contact the group and maybe get a cast."

On Tuesday I got back to my dream girl with script in hand, and again on Wednesday to learn about her feelings for the "Let's Go To College" story. I loved the warm welcoming mood of her upstairs apartment and the eager feminine way she pulled me into the room. I loved the rear window with its view into a neighbor's beautifully appointed garden. I loved everything about her little world.

Elsie's comments gave me a big boost. "It's good," she said. "I like it a lot. Of course, I'm not a writer. I read it as an actor. There are a few things I think would strengthen it."

Together we worked at revision for an hour, and then I took the marked-up pages back to my typewriter. On Thursday night at last I met the whole group. Instantly I had a cast, half a dozen young actors hungry for any opening that might lead to a job. One of them even had contact with a recording studio that would help to put the story in a form to peddle to radio stations.

Elsie became my chief producer-helper, and I became her chief spiritual inspiration. Together Elsie and I and the cast worked our way through February and March into April with excellent professional progress and high idealism. Steadily the cast grew more and more dedicated to the project.

Day after day I longed to take Elsie into my arms and was baffled as to why I could make no progress to overcome her walls against romance. My only clue came from an overheard remark Elsie made to one of the girls of the cast. She declared that so-and-so didn't have a chance because he was a "mama's boy." She hadn't been talking about me, but her judgment lit in my mind a tiny worry-flame that kept burning, on and on.

Early in May a confirmation of my fears hit squarely. An actor named Freddie came into the group to add his talents to the struggling cast. He had dash and daring and charm by the bucketful; all the things I didn't have. He was debonair, handsome and physical. Certainly no "mama's boy." I stood by, helpless, watching Elsie's walls collapse under Freddie's assaults.

Within the week it was all "touchie-touchie." The comfortable sofa in Elsie's apartment became a wrestling mat of sorts. I couldn't stand their constant horseplay. Tickling and giggling and kissing were at the top of their repertory, which was played to extremes until they came up for air, red-faced and sweating. The two of them didn't even seem to be aware of a third party presence. I stiffly sat in a chair and watched and squirmed.

Fortunately I had big responsibilities with the radio script and didn't have time to mope. Also, there were other forces at work in my life. Mother and I had come to West Hollywood with only that $100 in hand, and as it dwindled along the way and finally vanished, I was forced to get into part-time work with Don. The modest business in landscape maintenance in Beverly Hills was a godsend, and he and I worked well side by side. During my toddler years I had called him "Donald Daddy," for he cared for me with better sense than my father, then into his feeble seventies.

In mid-July, the thirteenth of the month to be exact, the unforeseen happened. Daryl, the actor in the cast who provided the recording studio contact and who also acted as informal agent to take our transcriptions to radio stations, got me on the phone.

"Herb, here's your report on marketing the 'College' series. Good news and bad news. My friend the manager loves the story. He thinks it will fly. The bad news: the whole industry has slipped into an economic nose dive and so he can't touch it."

"I thought Roosevelt's New Deal was supposed to take care of that," I pleaded.

"For sure," he said. "This is just the latest chapter of the Depression, or something like that."

"Well, gee, if your friend can't touch it, isn't there someone else?" A chill began to penetrate my bones.

"You didn't hear me. I said, 'the whole industry.' Nobody is going to gamble on anything new."

"Then what can we do?"

"We're dead."

I grabbed for a straw. "But it won't last forever."

"Six months. Maybe a year. I know this is hardest on you, Herb, but as far as I'm concerned the smart thing to do now is to put it on the shelf."

Next to Elsie, I had counted on Daryl most of all. Now my life really took a tailspin. I retreated to my sofa-bed, but sleep became torture. Nightmares of Elsie and Freddie got all mixed up with the wreckage of my artistic career. Next morning I told Don I didn't feel well enough to go to work. Don thought I looked all right, but he didn't know the earth had dropped out from under his brother. He went off to do the gardening jobs alone.

Luckily Mother had an appointment with a friend in downtown Los Angeles. I didn't crawl back into bed but sat alone on the sunshiny porch of the garden cottage and stared at the profusion of daisies and snapdragons that filled the eight-by-ten "front yard." The latest edition of "Variety" rested on my knees unread, meaningless.

Every step, up to that moment, had encouraged my dream for a drama career. But now the dream shattered against the hardrock reality of the world of business. On the porch I thought long about my dream girl, Elsie, and my love for drama. Somewhere, obviously, I had missed the right road.

Slowly the deeper current of feelings about independence and manhood swept through my spirit. Once again a touch of anger flared in my heart, that I continued to be tightly bound to Mother and economically dependent on Don. After six months I still hadn't broken away. Every succeeding day would be a postponement. I had to act. I had to tell my childhood and adolescence to get lost—now! Gradually a new vision brushed aside the broken bits of my artistic career.

Following supper, after I had cleared and washed the dishes, I came back to the table, pushed aside the messy pages of the L.A. Times that Don had just finished. I laid out my new thinking and watched with the sharpness of a poker player as Mother and Don reacted with a mixture of amazement and shock.

"I feel as though I've come to a dead end," I said. "There's no future for me in Hollywood. I think I'll go back to school."

"And give up gardening?" Don moaned. "Just when we're beginning to make a good income!"

"Manicuring Beverly Hills lawns isn't going to lead anywhere. I mean for me. Not at forty cents an hour. For you it's good. It's your business. I've got to get prepared for my own life."

Mother cross-examined with the seeming objectivity of a courtroom judge. "Do you mean to give up playwriting?"

"Only temporarily," I said. I had told her only little bits about the problems with the "College" series. I knew she was sympathetic with my artistic aspirations, but only up to a point. I knew she understood perfectly that monetary rewards, at best, would be far down the road ahead. And money was important to her, for she would soon arrive at sixty-five with no retirement income anywhere in sight other than her two boys.

"Then what would you do with more schooling?" said Mother.

"I would like to go back to Cal and study to become a soil scientist, especially in hydroponics. You know, water culture. It's a new field. There are some really good jobs waiting." I pushed quickly on while the surprise quality of my plan held center stage. "Mom, I think you should stay here with Don. Keep house for him for the present. I know it will be nip and tuck for me, odd jobs, student life, and all that. But I'll be all right, out on my own, for a while. You'll do a lot better here, and if I earn any extra money I'll send some to help out."

Mother didn't protest verbally. She left her seat to fuss with shelving dishes. I knew I had hit the mark. I had started something brand new between us: the obedient, loving mama's boy was talking like a convincing man of the world.

"Look, I know this is going to be hard for all of us," I pled with all the urgency I could muster, "but soil science is a logical extension of my A.B. degree in geography, and a very natural follow-up of my working in landscape soils with Don."

The deeper truth I kept to myself. This was the desperately real moment to make my break, to declare my independence, regardless of later consequences with Mother. My mind was made up.

I phoned Elsie, told her about Daryl's report, and that I had decided to go back to Berkeley. She was properly sad about the demise of our project, and lavished on me the same wonderful warmth I had felt during our first meeting in her apartment. It was too much. I hurried into my remaining formalities

"I promise I'll write," I said, "as soon as I get settled."

"Oh, yes," she said. "We must keep in touch."

But I felt in my guts that this was the end. I would probably never see her again. I hung up.

On the fifteenth of July I boarded the Southern Pacific Daylight to escape to the Bay area. I headed sturdily toward my new world of independence unaware that I had set loose a flood of events that would change my life forever and sweep me into the arms of a girl named Margaret.

Preacher's Kid
(1934-38)

"I want to withdraw my membership from the church!"

This was the rebellious announcement that I, daughter of the Rev. Ralph Waddell, flung at my father, as I confronted him in his study upstairs in the Petaluma parsonage. A college sophomore, I had returned from Berkeley for Christmas vacation, 1934.

If Daddy felt shock or annoyance he gave no sign. Calmly, he turned his swivel chair away from the roll-top desk so he could face me more directly. I sat tensely on my hard wooden chair, awaiting the response.

"And why do you want to do that?" he asked, with a slight lift of the eyebrows.

I blurted out my resentments that had been simmering over many weeks and had now reached the boiling point. "When I was swept into joining the church at the age of twelve, along with my whole Sunday School class, I didn't know what I was doing! I've been *indoctrinated* with Christian concepts of Jesus and God, and I accepted them without really thinking. I want to find the truth for myself, with inner authority."

I paused, breathless. How would Daddy—the source of much of this indoctrination—take my revolt? Would he feel hurt?

He did not seem disturbed. "Well, Margie, before a child is able to think things out for himself, it is best to have 'indoctrination' of a good sort, because he will be influenced in some direction by his peers or the environment anyway. When he is old enough to think for himself, then he can re-evaluate what he's been taught."

I fiddled with a button on my blouse. "That's what I've been doing, and I'm getting some different ideas." How could I tell him about my wonderful new visions of spirituality? During the past year, I had so often had an ecstatic feeling of being really alive. I had become keenly aware of the difference between helter-skelter "ordinary" living and "real" living, where the ultimate wonder and mystery of existence lifted me into amazed joy.

Trying to overcome my shyness, I ventured gently, "Sometimes I have a kind of mystical feeling that I am a soul." Could he know what I was talking about? I picked up with my protesting tone of voice. "The Sunday School never taught us about that. Most church members don't appear to know anything about mysticism. They just go through the forms."

Patiently my dad shared his own thinking about these matters. "You have to have forms and concepts in order to communicate anything," he pointed out. "I always try to see through the forms to the substance behind them. My task as a preacher is to use traditional forms, but put vitalizing substance into them, so people *will* be led to get meaning out of them."

I wasn't sure he'd been successful in that effort. "*I* don't get any inspiration out of the church!" I declared. "And I don't know enough about Jesus to promise undying allegiance to him." I averted my eyes to the glowing gas heater that warmed the room. "I'm not enthusiastic about spreading Christianity, the way a church member should be. So I don't think I should stay in the church."

Finally Daddy smiled and said, "All right. It's O.K. with me if you withdraw."

Unaware of the irony that I needed his approval for my "revolt," I felt relieved at having obtained it. I left the study and danced lightly down the stairs.

But we had not counted on Mother's reaction! The next morning in his study, my father pleaded with me. "Mother is very upset over the thought of your cancelling your church membership. I tried to explain your point of view, but she was in tears, almost hysterical. Church means a lot to her. Could you reconsider?"

I was disappointed, but I was not completely heartless. "O.K, I'll let the matter ride," I said resignedly. "But I'm withdrawing in spirit, anyway!"

In all this argument with Dad, and in similar discussions before and after, I had much support from a spiritual comrade I had discovered. William, Wim for short, was a fellow rebel who reinforced me in my unconventional stands, and pushed me even further.

Both of us had grown up in the Oakland church that my father served before his transfer to Petaluma, but I had never paid much attention to Wim. His curly dark hair, his prowess at debating, and his meticulous handwriting did not impress me. He was just a sort of "boy next door."

But circumstances threw us together as I became the first passenger in a simple car pool he and his brother Fred ran. They picked me up daily at the home where I now boarded, and I paid five cents for each ride from Oakland to the University of California in Berkeley.

While Fred drove, Wim often read to me from poems or prose that had especially struck him. One day it was from Longfellow: "Life is real! Life is earnest!...Let us then be up and doing..." Those words seemed to express what *we* felt, and an outlook that average church people failed to exhibit.

One morning their car was late in arriving. When at last it drew up to the curb, Wim got out and held the front door open gallantly. Fred shouted, "Sorry we're late! We had a flat tire!"

I took my usual seat in the middle, between the two boys. Wim was holding a large book, and his big grin suggested some special excitement. As soon as we were on our way, he burst out, with fire in his eye, "You've got to read this, Margaret!"

I took the heavy volume in my hands, and opened it to the title page. "'Cosmic Consciousness' by Richard Maurice Bucke," I read aloud. "Never heard of him. What's it about?"

Wim plunged in with enthusiasm. "Bucke outlines three kinds of consciousness: Simple consciousness, like the animals; self-consciousness, like most human beings; and cosmic consciousness, an exalted state that a few human beings have experienced."

I thumbed through the pages, catching a name here and there. "Oh! Buddha, and Jesus...Dante...William Blake.... You mean, the thing that made these guys special was that they had this cosmic consciousness?"

"Yes! And most of all, he says this shows the next stage in the evolution of the human race."

I was intrigued. "Can I borrow it?"

"Well, I promised I'd give it back today to the guy I got it from, Herb Dimock. But you can probably get a copy from the library."

The name he mentioned meant nothing to me at the time. Anyway, I was wrapped up in this deeply satisfying friendship with Wim.

Bucke's book, which I devoured late into the nights, enthralled me. I could accept Jesus better as part of a class of persons, instead of as one unexplainably wonderful individual. The notion that gradually more and more people would experience the higher consciousness kindled within me the lofty hope that I myself might become one of them. Aiming for "cosmic consciousness" became my new creed, and Wim's too.

The "Tuesday Night group," which Wim introduced me to, became my substitute for formal church services. Sitting around a fireplace in the Presbyterian student center (courtesy of the "church," which most of us felt estranged from!), this small circle of earnest young people shared aspirations and inspirations, and encouraged one another in working for peace and social justice. I came to feel a warm kinship with them all, and was especially glad for this new level of contact with Wim.

He had also persuaded me to take a class in Social Institutions with him. We sat in chair-desks, side by side, under Professor Teggart, on the second floor of Wheeler Hall. The professor waved his arms dramatically, and kept the whole class alert and uncertain as he carried the torch for a unique theory of human progress. Wim and I whispered comments to each other, as we poked holes in Teggart's philosophy.

At the end of one session, while chairs scraped and students made their exit, I was still jotting down notes on the lecture. Wim excused himself. "I'm supposed to meet a fellow in the hall. See you later."

When I loaded my arms with my big three-ring binder and two textbooks and picked up my sweater, I emerged from the classroom into the wide, echoing corridor. I saw Wim talking with a tall young man, and hesitated, wondering whether their conversation was private.

Wim caught sight of me, and beckoned me over. He told the stranger who I was, and then said to me, "This is Herb Dimock."

I'd heard the name before, but couldn't quite remember where. "Hi," was all I said to the gangly, mild-mannered fellow with slicked-back hair and a rather pasty complexion.

I stood there a few minutes, long enough to hear Wim tell Herb he ought to take Teggart's class. Herb shrugged his shoulders rather arrogantly, and said, "Nah—I don't need to. I could just read the book and take it credit-by-exam."

There was no point in my hanging around. "Nice to have met you," I said formally. "I have to get on to my next class."

I loved being with Wim anywhere—in classes, at parties and songfests of the Tuesday night gang, on committees to work for peace.

On his part, he appeared to enjoy my company, though he never really said so. His oblique way of asking me for a date was simply, "Oh, by the way, Margaret, if you don't object strenuously, I'll be dragging you to the dance on Friday."

I laughed, pleased, and answered in the same light mode. "O.K., if you insist."

Following my nineteenth birthday in the spring of 1935, our friendship began to shift into romance. I was unprepared for handling this new stage. In high school I had scoffed at "boy-crazy" girls. No one ever sought dates with me. Did they think a "preacher's kid" would be too prim and prissy? I didn't think of myself that way, but I did count it a virtue that I "took life seriously." I never flirted.

But now, on a Saturday in May, Wim telephoned me. I stood on one foot and then the other at the boarding house phone, while he raved on and on about a movie he had seen the night before, "Naughty Marietta." With no idea what he was driving at, I kept answering with comments like, "It sounds good," or "I'll have to see it."

"I'd sure like to see it over again," he said. Finally he got around to the purpose of his phone call. "Would you like to go with me—tonight?"

I quickly let go of my plans to catch up on studying. "That would be wonderful."

I had a date! But I didn't dare let myself become like those frivolous high school girls. I wouldn't dress up as though this was something special. I'd just wear the same cotton print dress I had put on that morning.

When Wim called for me, I excused myself from the boarding house dinner table to get my coat.

"You haven't eaten your apple pie yet!" one of the boarders called out.

I smiled, and left with Wim. Apple pie, which I loved, had become the lowest of priorities.

We didn't hold hands in the movie theater, although I was glad that our upper arms and shoulders touched now and then. When Nelson Eddy and Jeanette MacDonald sang, "I'm Falling in Love with Someone," I thought, "That seems to be true of us." But I was too shy to glance at Wim to see if he thought so too.

His light squeeze around my shoulders, when he delivered me at my door, put me in seventh heaven.

I did a lot of day-dreaming about Wim in the days that followed. But I held myself back. In my diary I wrote,

> I put a little too much emphasis on thinking about him this morning.
> Too much of that is a kind of self-indulgence. Because the real "sweet
> mystery of life" is something broader and wider.

That holding back still influenced me on a fair day in June when Wim drove me into the Oakland hills for a hike. From time to time, as I climbed the rocky trail, I realized his gaze was fixed on me with unusual interest. I was flattered, but it made me feel self-conscious. To lift my thoughts to "higher things," I focused my attention on seeing God in the beauties of nature. When we paused by a murmuring brook, I waved my hand toward a group of leafy trees. "Isn't that a lovely scene?"

His smiling reply took me off guard. "I'm more interested in the immediate foreground." He turned me around to face him, and drew me into his arms.

"Is this what it's like?" I wondered. Where was the ecstasy I had day-dreamed about?

My face looked across his shoulder, and I could feel his heart thumping. But my mind had been elsewhere, and I couldn't seem to pull myself into the present moment. He had to say, "I am going to kiss you," before I realized that was coming next. The kiss was not unpleasant, but I continued to feel stiff and wooden.

Letters flew back and forth between us all summer when I was home in Petaluma. He sent me his picture. I wrote him a sentimental poem. That's what lovers were supposed to do, wasn't it? We both wrote terms of endearment we had never spoken aloud.

Being "in love" was exhilarating and delightful, but I was frequently haunted by a shadow, a feeling that it all seemed "unreal." I trusted that my vague distress would eventually clear up. Time ahead seemed infinite.

With my return to college in the fall, our daily friendship seemed outwardly as wonderful as ever. I didn't realize that something different was developing.

One morning late in October the bomb fell.

I sat with Wim on the University lawn near the library, enjoying to the full our discussion of ethics, perfection, reincarnation.

And then he said, "There's something else we've got to talk about." He shifted his position uncomfortably. "I don't know just what to say—it's about me and Kay."

"Why? What about it?" I asked bluntly. Kay was a member of the Tuesday night group, and a good friend of mine.

He began pulling up little tufts of grass. "I don't know what's happened. We've been going out evenings, and...seeing quite a lot of each other... and..." His voice trailed off.

I was stunned. He couldn't possibly mean what it sounded like, could he?

I waited for him to explain further, but he went on pulling up grass. At that moment the bells of the Campanile sounded the hour for his next class, and he mumbled, "I've got to go."

I went to my Labor Econ class in a daze. I could barely pay attention to the lecture. I kept wondering, "What did he mean?" By evening I had to admit to myself that I might possibly lose him. The wrenching pain I felt made my love for him suddenly very, very "real."

Throughout the following weeks, my mind and emotions were in tumult. I was never able to come right out and ask Wim directly to clarify his fumbling announcement. He never brought up the subject himself.

My boarding house was now in Berkeley, within walking distance of the campus, so there were no more "car pool" rides together. But we continued to see a lot of each other, in the Tuesday Night gang, and in several classes. I felt overwhelming love, again and again, as I watched the firelight on his face at a picnic, or saw his eyes light up, brown and smiling, as he talked enthusiastically to me or to others about the love and joy at the heart of the universe.

Wim always remained friendly to me—just as he was with all our gang. At the same time, I knew he had special dates and projects with Kay. I alternated between heart-ache and hope.

I was not one to "wear my heart on my sleeve." My parents never knew my deepest feelings in this period. I talked with my friends and roommates about everything under the sun, but never about my affection for Wim or my bewilderment over what was happening. I shared my woes with nobody—except God.

At night, with hot tears falling on my pillow, I prayed. "God, what are you doing? Can't you turn things around? The way I want it seems so strong and inevitable and rooted in my heart! Can't you make it happen?"

But who was I to say what God intended? I knew that God's purposes and wisdom were far beyond my ability to understand. I saw the whole complex "situation" between Wim and Kay and me as not simply the actions and choices of us as individual persons, but as guided by the creative forces of the Universe itself.

In the spring, several of us from the Tuesday Night group signed up for "English 153B" under Professor Kurtz. When I walked into the classroom, the sight of Wim and Kay sitting cozily together in the second row sent an arrow of pain through my soul. My dim hopes crashed once again, and I stumbled toward a chair in the fourth row. I barely noticed Herb Dimock drifting into the room and taking the vacant seat on the other side of Wim.

Kurtz's own title for his course was "Captains of Turmoil." As he lectured about the *Iliad*, he pointed out how life is full of turmoil (mine certainly was!), and how no one could expect to be spared. With a triumphant flash and gleam in his eyes, he challenged us all to learn how to embrace and transcend it. I began to feel I could do so.

By the time Wim and Kay announced their engagement, I had come through my turmoil and felt truly happy for them both. Soon they were married, and moved to New York City.

I felt sure I would never find another partner like my "first love." But I had learned that to love could be richly fulfilling, even if one did not receive the same kind of love in return. That was enough.

Wim's departure meant not only the end of the chapter as far as our romance was concerned; it also meant a lessening of my dependence on him for my ideas and points of view.

When I first spilled out to my father my anti-church rebellion, that night in Petaluma, I had said I wanted to find the truth for myself. But did I find the "inner authority" I sought? No! I found myself taking Wim as an authority! I echoed his opinions about nearly everything—literature, churches, pacifism, the economic system. Then whenever he changed his stand, I was left hanging. I saw what I was doing, and in my diary I fumed over and over, "I *will* be my own authority. I *will* stand on my own feet." But I seldom succeeded.

With Wim no longer around to influence me, I tended to turn again to the person who had been my gentle authority through childhood, my father. Although I still felt strong opposition to table grace, hymn words, rituals, and churches in general, I began to see good sense in some of my dad's opinions.

He frequently reminded me that scholarships and the "parental purse" could not carry me forever, and I knew that was true. But my efforts to choose a "life work" had been fuzzy for a long time. I fantasized about "going down in the slums," becoming one with the poor and outcast.

One day Daddy said, "I talked with Miss Ballard, of the Board of Home Missions. They need someone to assist in running a vacation school for children of the cannery workers in Sunnyvale. Would you like to do that?"

I hesitated. Under Home Missions? A church agency? Me? But it would be a concrete opportunity to help the poor and oppressed. And at least it wasn't foreign missions, which I didn't approve of.

"All right. I guess I might as well," I agreed.

My month in the San Joaquin Valley helping Lila, a young Baptist woman, was absorbing and rewarding. I was glad to bring a few happy hours into the lives of the ragged, eager little children. Then a contact with a compassionate social worker in the Petaluma area led me finally to prepare for the profession of social work. Here was a field I could feel comfortable with, outside the church.

I entered the graduate Curriculum in Social Service at the University of California in the fall of 1937, and plunged into a new set of studies: Public Welfare, Mental Hygiene, Statistics, Jurisprudence.

Under the National Youth Administration (NYA), a New Deal agency, I earned $25 a month typing in the Curriculum office. On onion-skin paper, seven copies at a time, I typed long sections from a text-book on the Poor Laws of England, to be handed out to classes on Poverty. (No Xerox machines then, much less computers and printers!) The year sped by.

In the summer of 1938, my father accepted a new post on the staff of a big church in Los Angeles, and the family moved to an apartment there. I would be "on my own" more than ever, now, for visits home would be rare. I felt good about my increasing independence.

When I returned to Berkeley for my second year of social service training, I sought out Ricky, one of the girls I had shared an apartment with the previous spring. "Have you found a place for us for this year?"

"Yes," Ricky told me excitedly. "It's just half a block from the campus, on the fourth floor, and it has a wonderful view."

She took me to see it. Though it was small, its fresh paint and wallpaper made it attractive. "I guess we can manage to fit five of us in," I said dubiously.

The next day we all gathered in the apartment to make plans about furniture. Harriet had some news: "The landlord found out we invited Oriental friends to visit us last year. He told me we couldn't have this place after all!"

I was shocked. "What prejudice! Did you try to change his mind?"

"Well, he said if we would promise not to invite any Orientals or Negroes, he might yield."

Did a couple of the girls seem to be wavering? I surely felt confused about a lot of social issues, but not about this one. "We can't do that!" I stated with more than usual vehemence. I thought of my dear Chinese American friend, Grace. "How could I look Grace Tow in the face and tell her we had made such a promise?"

The girls squirmed. One said, "But it's so close to the campus, and has such a great view!"

I argued hotly, "If we preach that other people should sacrifice for their ideals, we ought to be willing to give up some of those things"

My strenuous objection finally carried the day. We found a new place on Grove Street, a few blocks west, a whole lower flat, furnished, for $35 a month. By the time we moved in, there were seven of us.

After lunch the next Saturday, I set out for the campus to study in peace and quiet. As I walked up University Avenue in the refreshing Berkeley air, I smiled with satisfaction over our housekeeping arrangements. Each girl had agreed to put in $2 a week for food. Besides that, Tom and Wayne, whom some of us knew, would pay at the same rate to eat dinners with us.

I crossed Oxford Street and started up the curving sidewalk at the west edge of the campus. Coming toward me I saw a tall fellow wearing a hat. His gait looked familiar. Why, it was Herb Dimock! I hadn't seen him since he graduated two years ago.

"Hi, Herb!" I greeted him as he came closer. "You back on campus?"

We carried on casual, polite conversation, and then my interest in providing more money for our food kitty led me to ask, "Do you have a place to eat?"

"Yes," he said, "I get my meals at the Ivanhoe, where I have a job waiting tables."

I made one more pitch. "Well, if you ever need to make a change, you might consider eating dinners at our co-op. Seven of us girls have a flat at 1911 Grove St."

"Thank you," Herb answered non-committally. "I'll remember that."

And we went our separate ways.

Plucking Daisy Petals
(1938-39)

We try to explain away special happenings in our human experience as "just coincidences." As I look back, the crossing of my path with Margaret's on the curving road down to Oxford was a "divine" coincidence, for without that casual moment our paths might never have touched again.

On that particular day, with the most transcendent irony imaginable, I was intent on catching a trolley that would take me to the rooms of another woman in neighboring Alameda.

My relocation from Los Angeles to Berkeley had laid on me the heavy urgency to find work to feed and house myself and to save enough for the modest registration fees at the University. A job waiting tables at the rambling Victorian retirement Hotel Ivanhoe took care of the food. For the rest I renewed contact with my old friends at the Department of Geography: Doctors Sauer, Leighley and Kesseli. I hired on as part-time cartographer to draw maps for Sauer's field research near Oaxaca, Mexico. I did charts for economist Dr. Daggett, covering the market for oranges shared by Florida, Texas and California.

In almost no time at all I established my economic base and was able to relax and enjoy my world. The beauty of the University of California campus took possession of my soul again. I rejoiced in the ancient trees, the rambling paths, Strawberry Creek with its somersaulting, gurgling run down toward the Bay. I had come back to my intellectual and emotional home, the place of promise for the future.

And then early one Friday afternoon Mrs. Wells, the secretary of the Department, called to me as I worked in the geography library.

"Phone call for you, Herb."

I stepped into her adjacent office. "Who is it?"

"A girl."

I took the receiver with puzzlement. "Hello?"

"It's your long lost you-know-who."

"Elsie! Where are you?"

"Alameda."

"Oh my God! You're here! What's up?"

She spilled out her long sad tale. Freddie had fled to New York to pursue his stage career, and she couldn't stand the yakking of her mother. She wanted to touch base with me, so she had come north and stayed with her aunt in Alameda until she found her own apartment.

"Well, gee, when can I see you?" I begged.

Something new, I felt, something very new was beginning to happen between us. Elsie had uprooted herself from Hollywood, even as I had. She was lonely, as I was. For the first time I sensed in her what could only be called an aura of seductiveness. My romantic pulse beat with more hope than I had ever before dared. Is she telling me I have a chance?

We made a date for the weekend, for me to come to her apartment. On Saturday I left my work headquarters at the Department with my heart full. Now that Freddie was out of the way, everything had changed. I was dreaming what every young man expected in those days, that maybe I was going to find THE somebody with whom I could build my own family... Elsie.

In Alameda at a nearby nursery, I bought a beautiful potted geranium with a single red bloom standing proudly above the dark, green foliage. At about three o'clock I knocked at Elsie's door and presented my gift. She didn't throw herself into my arms, as I hoped she might, but her delight with my floral offering made the beginning of our reunion wonderfully worthwhile. Hand-in-hand we went shopping at a store down the street, and I dug into my pocket to pay for our supper materials. Side by side we cooked the meal in her two-bit kitchenette, and with lighted candles on the table and classical music on her phonograph, we broke bread together and indulged in our favorite talk about things spiritual. Late in the evening, heedless of all practical realities, I made my overture.

"Elsie, do you suppose we should get married?" My choice of words was absolutely weird, but her smile glossed over my naivete.

Softly, she said in effect she was willing to consider my proposal. "Be patient. We'll see."

Never once had we shared a kiss, and not even now. My whole body yearned for an embrace, but she didn't make the faintest move to encourage me. I simply was not the aggressive lover who would take things into his own hands. I went back to my campus world to wait for developments.

Along about Halloween, Kesseli referred me to a tutoring job for a sophomore co-ed who had failed Geography One and had to take it over. At the time I was simply glad for any job that would put more money in my pocket. I had not the vaguest clue that this unsought-after, even casual opportunity, amounted to a fork in the road for me.

Over the Christmas holidays between semesters, Dr. Sauer left the Department on Guggenheim Foundation business, and John Leighly became acting chairman. Dr. Leighly was the best of mentors to me, my top friend in academia. Because of him, in my senior year, I had been hired as the University's official weather observer. He was the one who taught me the fine points of cartography and steered me into many jobs as map maker. In a way he was more of a father to me than my own father had ever been.

Several days before Christmas, Leighly called me into his second floor office in Hilgard Hall. My confidence was high. I had earned straight A's in my first semester courses. My physical well-being was the best in many moons. I wore a new thrift-shop jacket that concealed some of the slump of my shoulders. My cream-colored corduroy pants were freshly laundered.

I pushed open the office door. The winter sun shone through venetian blinds to direct a floodlight of approval on the University's only professor of meteorology. A big smile curved the sides of his mouth as he broke his news to me.

"Herb, we have an opening for a teaching assistant. The enrollment for Kesseli's Geography One is going to be much bigger than expected. Would you be interested?"

I gulped. I had never imagined myself in a T.A. role. Professors and teachers of all shades belonged to another world beyond my ken. Also, I was shy in those days, expecting others to initiate conversation and provide leadership. I was Herbie, the listener. Herbie, the follower. Still, I knew I had turned in an excellent job with my co-ed tutoree, and this T.A. job offered a passport to the stars.

"Yes, sir! I certainly would be interested." Strange how one little "yes" can change a person's entire life.

I couldn't wait to phone Elsie about my great good fortune. She seemed much impressed with my upward climb at the university, and we promised each other that we would get together as soon as possible. But first I had to make a trip back home for Christmas and share my success with Mother and Don.

What I discovered in West Hollywood wasn't good. In the one bedroom of the tiny garden cottage, Mother lay stretched out, obviously in pain. She had suffered a fall. I sat close on the edge of the bed and held her hand.

"What is it?" I asked.

She pointed me to the top of the chest of drawers where I found a large envelope with an X-ray of her neck. "Look at the third vertebra," she said. "It's broken. Doctor says I've got to wear a heavy leather collar."

"Leather collar? Where is it?"

"Too expensive. We can't afford the thirty-five dollars."

That's when I told her about my new T.A. job, and she was wonderfully glad for me. I vowed to send money from my expanded income, to help with the collar price. I also determined to write to Uncle Don, Mother's older brother, and urge him to help out. I realized that my best service in the emergency would be to stick to my job.

I returned to Berkeley and prepared to move into the office I would share with other T.A.s. The semester began and I carried a full load of classes, but course work occupied the back seat in my priority system. The demands of my teaching job swept toward me like Dorothy's tornado in Kansas. Dr. Kesseli, my supervisor, was Swiss and spoke with a heavy accent, so thick most of the students missed the gist of his lectures. I had three sections twice a week, and at my first meeting with each the cry was loud— "What is the professor talking about?" I proceeded to give a rather full rehash of the lecture, and from that week on it was the same. I delivered, from my own extensive notes, "The Essence of Physical Geography a la Kesseli." Overnight, I became a very popular T.A.

The flush of pleasure stayed with me week after week as a string of students visited my office to seek extra help with the course. Without me the students would flounder their way toward inevitable F's at the end of the semester. At least that's the way it seemed. I enjoyed every minute.

My big leap in affluence that came with the modest T.A. salary enabled me to quit my job as waiter at the Ivanhoe, but that meant I needed a regular place to eat. The happy solution was immediately at hand. I remembered the invitation Margaret Waddell had given to join the eating co-op at 1911 Grove Street.

The house proved to be a gentle feminine chaos. They had a lower flat with a living room, kitchen, bedroom and bath. I never fully understood how seven girls crowded into that compact space without clawing each other to death.

We shared suppers around a big kitchen table, cramped on one side by a double bed. It served also as a study table. Piles of books and papers regularly had to be scooped off onto the bed to make room for our extremely simple meal, which included such hardly gourmet items as rice and split-pea soup and carrots and, quite often, cabbage, plus jello fancied up with chopped apples. But I didn't mind because the weekly cost was only two dollars per member. Everybody took turns at cooking chores and dishwashing.

Our table talk provided a big bonus for me, a break from soils and botany and geography. I listened, fascinated by the dominant theme, student anti-war activity. We all felt a growing anxiety about the aggressive behavior of Adolph Hitler as he made himself the dominant actor in Central Europe. Piece by piece he was carving up Czechoslovakia and pressuring Poland to yield to his territorial demands. We feared that the only possible outcome would be another European war, and our peace activists were very busy promoting American neutrality.

I found the Grove Street co-op to be an extremely dedicated bunch. One of the girls was a student at the Pacific School of Religion, two had a Congregational Church background, another taught in a Presbyterian Sunday School, and one said she was an atheist. There was a professed non-thinker who refused to indulge in the broad abstractions tossed around by the others. One of the male diners planned to be a missionary to India. They were definitely a religious group.

Within the first week of my joining I realized I had entered a new arena for the courting instinct that ran hot in my blood. I no longer had time to chase over to Alameda, and anyway Elsie kept up a mood of tension between us. But here in the co-op I had seven young women at close range with intimate daily contact at dinners!

I feasted on the physical presence of Mary, Lois, Harriet, Pat, Ricky, Serena, and at the bottom of the totem pole was Margaret. To me she seemed the plainest of the plain.

Of the three co-op "sisters" I looked at with a special gleam in my eye, Mary was already spoken for, Lois let me know gently that I was not her type. The third? Truly I never understood what Harriet saw in me, but we clicked.

Perhaps it was my teaching assistant job that seemed glamorous to her. She radiated allurement. Harriet had something indefinable that my starlet Elsie lacked. She came to my shared T.A. office in Ag Hall several evenings and sat across the table from me while I graded student quiz papers. She exuded a Mona Lisa smile with an exciting "come hither" look in her eyes, which I found hard to resist.

"Harriet..."

"Yes?" She looked up from her book, instantly available to me.

"Ah...I was just wondering. Would you like to go to the dance at Stevens Union Saturday night?"

"That would be nice."

"We can go right after supper."

"I should get home at a reasonable hour. I have my Sunday School class to prepare for."

"Sure. Of course." I groped eagerly for some way to enrich our apparent growing tie. "Say, would it be appropriate for me to visit your class?"

"Not really. They are eleven-year-old girls, full of bounce. You wouldn't have any fun."

"Oh. I see." I retreated from that dead end. "What are you studying?"

"I'm cramming for a Medieval History midterm."

When I finished my quizzes I played escort down University Avenue to Grove Street. We held hands all the way. I had initiated the same physical contact also with Mary and Lois whenever we shared a walk to or from the campus, but holding Harriet's hand was special. Somehow she transmitted a psychic, electric current of power to me that robbed me of objectivity.

Under the influence of the romantic fog that closed in around my mind, I determined that I simply must find out what was the difference between the two girls I had fallen in love with—Elsie and Harriet. "Well, Herb!" I said to myself, "You certainly know how to honor your friends!" Any right-minded person would say I was crazy.

My opportunity came soon because of a colossal goof with my dating calendar. Forgetting that I had promised to take Elsie to see a play at the Wayfarers Civic Repertory theater, I set up an evening with Harriet for the very same show. There was no escape. I had to take both.

We rode the Bay Bridge train to San Francisco and took a street car out to Van Ness and Clay. All the way our conversation clung to everyday superficialities.

"It's really foggy tonight," I said, testing the waters.

Harriet made light of it. "I've seen worse."

Elsie dredged up an old memory. "Did you say you once lived here?"

"Yeah. Just a couple of blocks from the theater."

With one half of my mind I chuckled at the bold competition I had set up, wondering if one would ace the other out in some way. With the other half I shuddered at the possibility that both of them would write me off. But the girls had their own wills and their own agenda. Neither one seemed motivated to develop a real contact with the other. They talked only with me, as though the other was not present.

The evening as a whole left me with continuing puzzles and doubts. I had hoped to find something in one or the other that would help me come closer to deciding on a life partner, for that is what I yearned for most passionately. Each in her own way was terrific. Elsie grabbed my emotions with her physical beauty and her sense of drama. Harriet appealed to me with her ideas and a wonderful magnetic coquettishness. I wanted an answer.

In less than a week after our Wayfarers adventure the scales tipped for me. It was another one of those long evenings in my T.A. office. Harriet sat there at her post opposite me, studying for some course. None of the other T.A.s were around, nobody to question us, nobody to watch. From time to time she flashed me her Mona Lisa bit. Finally I couldn't stand it, couldn't resist any longer, couldn't force my mind to stick to the quiz work before me.

"Let's go out for some fresh air," I suggested. She accepted my hand, and I led her out the back door of Ag Hall. We slipped softly into the foggy darkness to the west side of Hilgard Hall where the gentle pulse of Berkeley traffic three blocks away whispered to us, "Life is love, life is love!" There were lots of bushes to screen us. I held her face in my two hands. I stared into her liquid eyes. I took her into my arms. We kissed passionately.

"Will you marry me?" I blurted in a wild excess. I pushed over the final frontier in a big hurry, in a way I had not dared to do with Elsie. I frightened myself with my boldness. The clammy Berkeley air washed around my over-heated face.

Harriet's answer had all the promise of a dripping faucet. "I don't know, Herb."

I wanted to ask, when will you know? Instead we drifted back to my office, and then I walked her home to the Grove street bed she shared with one of the other "sisters."

At dinner the following day we touched hands with uncommon warmth, but in her eyes I could find no hint of an answer to my proposal, only a feeling that there was a space of uncertainty between us. We were friends, but she no longer came to my office in the evening. As day followed day, that spreading space between us became a gulf, an abyss, an emptiness that left me very much alone.

The next time I called Elsie for a date her answer was simple and direct. "Herbie, dear boy, I'm real busy. Sorry." I had plucked the petals from two daisies, and the answer in both was, "She loves me not." They had said it loud and clear, "Nice guy, but no thanks."

I turned back to work with my sections and my courses, and then swiftly the semester was over. Truly it had been a year of victory after victory, with my arms full of trophies —except for one. My prospects for marriage failed miserably. Was it simply that I had bumbled? Or was there something else? I pondered this deeply and finally told myself, "Yes, each of my two girl friends would have made good 'bed mates' and good 'head mates,' but I want more. I want a soul mate, and neither one really fills that role." I wasn't exactly sure what I meant by "soul mate." It was an image I had picked up from my mother, but I was sure I would know when I found the right one. I suffered a deepening loneliness. I did not understand how deep was my need to find a mate who could replace the family ties I had broken when I moved out on my own.

At the last dinner of the co-op there were fond farewells and great jollity. Margaret asked the whole group about who would be in town during the summer. "If anyone is interested," she said, "we could cook together and save money."

I didn't care particularly. I would be away during intersession on a six-weeks soil science field trip. And when I came back it would be the grind of summer session. I didn't want to think any further ahead.

I had come back to the U, driving toward a life work in science. All of my previous counsellors, from high school on, had pushed me in that direction, but no longer did science rule my heart, if ever it had. I had discovered a talent for teaching, a talent for counselling troubled students, for leadership. I had moved into a world where people were more important to me than things. I stumbled along in a strange limbo. I didn't know which way to turn.

For the time being it was soil science. I would hang on to that drag until I had to drop it.

After six weeks on the road, with a dozen other young men, we were back in Berkeley, and I dutifully enrolled in summer session. Organic Chemistry was an essential course for my science career, but something began to go drastically wrong. As I sat listening to the professor drone on about carbon compounds, the door to my mind slammed shut. I studied hard, as with every other course I had taken, but my brain clogged. I knew that if I didn't pass I would have no future in soils.

It was July 1939, the end of my "wonderful year," my first year on my own. My bid for independence seemed to be slipping from my grip. I was making a mess of it. Who am I, anyway? What am I good for? All the glamor of science turned to ashes. I certainly wouldn't have another chance at a T.A. job in the Fall if I turned in an F in chemistry. Herb, the charging knight in armor, was being reduced to serf. Would I be condemned to return to the soil of landscape maintenance? At forty cents an hour?

Summer session became a desert of Sahara proportions. Everybody was away on vacation: professors, students, friends. Everybody. I drifted, lonely, from my bachelor room, to classes, to my empty T.A. office, to cheerless restaurants.

I wanted someone to talk to. Anyone. And then came Sunday, July 9th. I remembered a letter that had come to me at one of our field trip stops. I dug among the envelopes of my shoebox filing system and found the one from Margaret. Two things flashed again: she told how, at Mary's suggestion, she, Mary, Lois and Harriet had visited my mother in Los Angeles, and how she expected to be back in Berkeley the first week of July to start her new job with the Alameda County Charities. I could inquire of her through Auntie Helen in Oakland. Her contact point.

Anything would be better than this gray existence in the basement of Ag Hall where the foggy sunshine barely seeped in through the tiny north-facing window. I went to the department phone and dialed.

"Hello, is Margaret there?...This is Herb Dimock.... She's in Berkeley?...Oh, very good. Her address?..."

Margaret had found a room on the south edge of the campus at 2340 Bancroft Way. Uncle Jack had driven her only an hour ago to move luggage into her new home. What the hell! I might as well check it out right now.

My walk across campus, on empty paths and lawns on that Sunday afternoon, gave me time to review. The picture of Margaret that floated into my mind was a caricature: straight dark hair, "rice-bowl" bob, dowdy clothing, a bookish co-ed with horn-rimmed glasses, the polar opposite of glamor. All of my association with the Grove Street co-op had only confirmed my judgment, including the one time when we saw each other at a dance in the Student

Union and I swung her around the floor in a waltz. I especially noted her plainness, how she seemed deliberately to avoid dressing herself with feminine artfulness.

But all of that did not dampen the fact that she had been interested enough to write me a letter, and that she and those other sisters had visited my mother. It would be worth a try.

I dodged across the Sunday afternoon traffic on Bancroft Way and climbed six steps to the porch of 2340. I rang the doorbell and waited, wondering.

Two Can Do It
(1939)

The jangle of the doorbell echoed through the big old house on Bancroft Way. Was I supposed to answer it? No one else seemed to be home, so I decided I'd better.

I opened the door, and there stood Herb.

"Hello, stranger!" he said, grinning.

"Herb!" I gasped. "How did you know where to find me?"

He joked. "A little bird told me."

I smiled at his winsome evasion. "Auntie Helen?"

"Yep."

His blue eyes seemed to be taking me in from head to toe. I was glad I was wearing my favorite dress, a flowered voile with ruffles at the neck, and that I had persuaded my hair to curl a little on the ends.

"Come on in! Let me show you my new quarters."

I led Herb down the dingy hall, past the locked door of the landlady's room, the bare dining room, and the closed door of another tenant. We came to the doorway of the back bedroom.

"This is mine." I waved toward the two iron cots, the bureau with a diagonal crack in its mirror, and my gaping half-unpacked suitcases. "I just found this place yesterday. Isn't it swell? Only twelve dollars a month, and with use of the kitchen. Here, I'll show you."

Herb looked with approval at the kitchen, with its big iron stove, small table, and two wooden chairs. An attached pantry held cupboard shelves and the sink.

"So this is where you're going to cook!" He paused, and looked at me uncertainly. "Uh...did you ever find anyone from the Grove Street co-op to cook and eat with you?"

"No," I answered matter-of-factly, "it seems no one is back in town yet. Except...how about you? Do you want to join me for dinners? It would save expense for both of us."

For a few seconds I could almost hear the wheels in his mind spinning. I sensed an eagerness in his answer. "Why not?" And then he blew me away with a further suggestion. "How about breakfasts, too?"

I gulped. "Well, sure...if you don't live too far from here."

"Actually, just half a block!" He motioned with his thumb.

I'd forgotten what a resonant, melodious voice he had. This new arrangement was going to be fun.

It was not until a few hours later—after we had shopped for groceries, shared a meal, and set the time to meet for breakfast—that I was overcome with astonishment: it had been fun, wonderful fun, more than I ever imagined!

I lay awake a long time that night. While cool air, fragrant from the garden of the Women's City Club across the back fence, wafted through the open window to touch my face, waves of amazement washed over me. I had to ask myself, "Am I falling in love with Herb?" How else account for my great gladness in seeing him? Why else would I have enjoyed doing those mundane things with him so much? And where else could these sweet new sensations bubbling up within me have come from?

My mind whirled with memories. At Grove Street I had paid no attention to Herb. He was simply a pleasant acquaintance. Only a few months ago, on my twenty-third birthday, I had lamented in my diary,

> Ah, me! I crave such a high type of person for a life-partner, and there are very few of them. I'm almost ready to accept the idea of always being an old maid. It would not be the worst thing in the world.

But now, something new!

In the broad daylight of the next morning, my rosy elation became muted. I cautioned myself, "You have no idea whether Herb feels the same way about you. Take it easy."

I went ahead and got dressed dutifully. I was combing my hair at the bureau when I heard a voice singing a familiar phrase from Gilbert and Sullivan's *Mikado*: "A wandering minstrel I, a thing of shreds and patches..." I caught sight of the top of Herb's head passing by my window on his way to the back door. A shiver of pleasure ran up my spine at his makeshift serenade. I threw down my comb and scurried through the kitchen to let him in.

Breakfast was companionable, but Herb gave no sign that he had been swept away by any great passion for me.

For two days, we carried on as planned. The other first-floor tenant hardly ever came around, so we had the kitchen all to ourselves. Every now and then, as we came close in cooking, I felt an unexpected strong physical attraction to Herb. I wondered whether he felt anything like it...or not.

I was glad that we continued to observe the Grove Street custom of silent moments before eating. That I could accept, though I still resisted the ritual of a spoken grace. I felt the silence drew us together in spirit.

But we kept our dinner conversations quite objective. I told him about the small grocery co-op recently started in Berkeley, of which I was a member. He told me how he had learned to use a "soil auger" on his soil science field trip. It bothered me that, too often, I found myself giggling self-consciously.

Wednesday night the ice began to break. "I got a letter from my mother today," Herb said at supper.

I looked up from my lentils and summer squash, pleased that he had brought up a more personal subject.

He continued, "You and the other girls went to see her in Los Angeles, didn't you? How was she doing?"

"Oh, I liked her a lot!" I said. "I could hardly believe she was almost sixty-five. She certainly is young in spirit." I refrained from mentioning my shocked surprise that she wore lipstick and rouge, and high heels —all of which I disdained to wear myself.

Instead I went on to say, "She served us cookies and lemonade in the garden, and read our palms. I liked her philosophy. She crushed a handkerchief in her hand, and then pulled the corners of it out between her fingers to show how all people are united underneath."

Herb smiled. "Yeh, that's one of her favorite examples."

I wasn't yet ready to report something else Martha Yale had said to us as we left her tea party: "Be good to my boy. He is very lonely." Was he still lonely, I wondered, now? He didn't need to be. I was there. Or hadn't he noticed?

While we washed dishes in the pantry, Herb told me how his mother had healed her broken neck earlier in the year. "She tried wearing a heavy brace," he said, "but it only increased her pain. She got disgusted with it and threw it into the closet. Then she lay on a couch, with her feet elevated, and devoted herself to inspirational reading and what she calls 'deep meditation.' She did that for ten days, and her neck was completely healed."

I was impressed. "That's remarkable. The meditation I keep trying to do is sure far below that level!"

"Me too," Herb sighed. "We have a long way to go, haven't we?"

His putting the two of us together in the same humble stage of earnest upreach warmed my heart. After our kitchen chores were finished, I was happy to hear him suggest we go for a walk. If we wanted a chance for further talk—and I certainly did—walking was about the only alternative, since my residence boasted no parlor, and it was the landlady's policy that I was not to entertain gentlemen in my bedroom.

Herb took my arm chivalrously as we crossed Bancroft Way, but let go as soon as we reached the curb. We walked north on Dana Street past the Men's

Gymnasium, and stepped onto a campus path under the oak trees. So far our conversation had been superficial. I cast about for some subject that would really help me get better acquainted with Herb.

By the time we wandered along the west end of the Life Sciences Building toward a eucalyptus grove, I spoke up. "There's something else your mother told me when I visited her," I ventured.

Herb looked into my face with immediate interest. "What's that?"

"She said she had a dream or a vision when you were born. Angels with trumpets, and a voice saying, 'Here at last is the World Teacher.'"

Herb stood stock still. "She told you that? Did she tell the other girls too?" His face was anxious.

"Oh, no! She invited me alone for a second visit. We talked about a lot of other things. But this, she said, was a secret, and I mustn't tell anyone."

He relaxed a little and we started walking again. "I'm surprised she even told you. It's kind of embarrassing."

I hadn't taken his mother's vision very seriously. I tried to reassure him. "She said it meant you would do something great for humanity. You want to do that, don't you?"

We had reached the circle of log benches among the eucalyptus trees. "Well, sure," Herb said as we sat down. "But she seemed to mean I would be like Jesus or Gautama, or Krishnamurti."

"That would make her feel real important, wouldn't it?" I said with sudden insight. When Herb made no response, I went on, "If not that, what kind of service to humanity do you want to give?"

His eyes narrowed into slits and he had a faraway look. "Something that would make a lasting mark on the collective life of man! That would bring social justice. That would turn people's hearts away from violence and war."

"That's what I want to do, too," I said earnestly.

"Through social work?" he asked.

"That's a place to begin," I granted. "In my present job I'm learning a lot about the hardships people on Old Age Assistance have to meet. I can help them a little. But I'm not sure I'll make a career of it. I've always wanted to be an author and a poet. My plan right now is to stick with this job for a year or so, and then see how I feel."

At the end of our first week of "cooperative housekeeping," as Herb called it, I wrote in my diary,

Oh, God, it's a wonderful feeling...this yearning toward unity, this urge to blend ones own life with another person's....

Gee, I watch him getting food ready or washing dishes, and just wish I could come up behind him and slip my arm around his waist and squeeze him. But that will come later...if it is to come. How will I ever be bold enough to say, "I love you"?

"Let's hike up to the Big C," Herb said a couple of evenings later. I nodded eagerly.

The "Big C" was a huge concrete letter lying flat on the steep hillslope. Its golden-yellow paint cried out to everyone on the Berkeley streets below that this was the "Cal" campus.

We walked up the hill behind the football stadium to our goal, and sat on the lower edge of the "C", our feet among the dry summer grasses and weeds. As we looked out over the lights beginning to twinkle in Berkeley and San Francisco, Herb opened up his central concern.

"Marge," he began, "I'm really at a crossroads in my life right now."

I was touched by the worry in his voice. "Crossroads?" I echoed.

"Yes. I think I'm going to flunk organic chem. I just can't seem to hack it."

I felt a moment of guilt for having been so wrapped up in my own romantic thoughts that I hadn't been aware he was having a tough time with his daily studies. I had assumed he always did well in his courses.

"My heart's just not in science," he went on. "But I don't know what to do instead!"

I listened spellbound as he described the various kinds of employment he'd had in the past: sheep ranch, cannery, post office, warehouse clerk, gardener, cartographer, weather observer.

"But none of those things grabs me for a permanent career," he said with downcast face.

My sympathy went out to him. "What do you really want to do?"

"Write plays!" He told me about his frustrated efforts in writing radio plays in Hollywood. "I know I can't make a living at that. Not any time soon."

I felt his distress so keenly that I was tempted to offer him half my fabulous $120/month salary as a "scholarship," to free him to write. A rather wild idea, since even my first pay check wasn't due for another two weeks, and I still had summer debts to pay.

"And then," he continued, kicking pebbles with his shoe, "if I should get married, I wonder what difference that would make. It would be a strait jacket under some conditions."

I leaped in with an affirmation that I tried to make sound casual. "I don't think it should make much difference." I meant to imply that marriage to me wouldn't be a strait jacket. I was unaware of the proposals of marriage he had already made to two other girls.

During our whole absorbing conversation there on the hillside, I felt very close to Herb, and at the same time very far from him. I wrote afterwards in my diary,

How little I know of Herb and all his struggles! I'm not at all sure I want to share my whole life with him. I'd need to know him more deeply before I'd be ready for that.

Divine providence surely led me through the day-by- day episodes that further unveiled to me this dear stranger. Even sour cream made its contribution!

We had no refrigerator, and when the cream we had poured from the top of our milk bottle turned sour, I asked him, "How do you use up sour cream?" In those days, we'd never heard of sour cream on baked potato or in "dips."

With a twinkle in his eye Herb answered, "That's one of the few things I know nothing about!"

I was tickled by his sense of humor. He did know a lot about many things: current events, science, history, even how to make muffins without a recipe. But since he could poke fun at his own abilities, I concluded he was not really so arrogant as our first meeting several years ago had suggested.

On one of our nightly strolls another piece of his history slipped into view. We had proceeded several blocks up Bancroft Way when we passed a large Victorian house on our right. "That's where Miss Hilgard lives," Herb said with a wave of hs hand.

"Miss Hilgard?" I wasn't sure I had heard of her before.

"The lady who praised the play I wrote for Professor Kurtz' class."

"Oh yes, I remember." I was curious. "How did you happen to know her, anyway?"

He told me that it was her custom each year to give a significant graduation gift to "a deserving student who would not be recognized otherwise." In 1936, Herb's name had been proposed.

"And this is what she gave me." He pushed up the cuff of his brown jacket to show the Longines wrist watch I had noticed but never asked about. "When I went to her house to thank her, she took a real personal interest in me and my writing plans. It meant a heck of a lot to me."

On one meditative evening, I walked over to the Geography Building on campus with Herb. In a quiet room, I read a book on "Jesus" by Kahlil Gibran, while across the big table Herb studied for a chemistry exam. Every now and then he looked up and gave me a beautiful smile. I loved our comradeship.

On the walk home, we discussed our ideas of Jesus. "I've always been puzzled about the story of Jesus' being angry and driving the money changers out of the temple," I said. "And his lashing out at the Pharisees with 'Woe unto you, hypocrites.' Do you think he really did those things?"

"I don't know," Herb said thoughtfully. "I think we can choose what parts of his teachings we want to focus on. Like 'love your enemy.'"

"And 'Father, forgive them,'" I chimed in. I was glad to see we had a similar outlook.

The next day I began my diary entry with a kind of apostrophe to his mother:

> Ah, Mrs. D., your darling son is not quite a world leader—yet. He's a dear sweet gentle fellow, still kinda shy and scared in many respects, but with something there—a seeking and striving upward... He needs to have a partner who can disarm him of shyness, and grow with him.

I went on to add my self-analysis:

> I feel more like a mature woman than I was three years ago. I'm more ready for this experience.

The following Sunday afternoon found me on top of the world—literally! I stood with Herb on a rock at the summit of Mt. Tamalpais enjoying the view of much lower landscapes in all directions, including the whole of San Francisco Bay. The breeze tossed my hair and fluttered my flowered voile dress, and Herb took a picture of me with his Voigtlander camera.

My heart was full of joyful gratitude for the twenty-four hours just past. Herb and I had come to Fairfax, in Marin County, at the invitation of my parents. My father was supply-preaching in the Congregational church there during his vacation.

As I stood on the mountain top, scenes from the weekend flashed through my mind: Herb's fascinated expression as he greeted my minister father, Ralph, and my cheerful mother, Peggy. The warm acceptance which my parents gave Herb. The silly "fooling around" that went on between my sister Lois, three years younger than I, my fourteen-year-old sister Shirley, and Herb and me. Herb's clowning with a German accent all Saturday evening, to the giggles of us girls. Mock contests over who grabbed the Sunday morning funny papers first. Attendance at Ralph's church service, to which Herb and I conformed courteously, and found it "not too bad." Herb's obvious appreciation of the delicious Sunday dinner Peggy prepared.

All through those encounters and activities, I was delighted that Herb kept taking hold of my hands or touching my shoulders. Best of all, as Daddy drove all of us up Mt. Tamalpais, Herb's left arm, casually draped along the back of the seat, drifted down onto my shoulders. Our hands groped for each other. No wonder I felt on top of the world!

During our trip back to Berkeley by ferry and bus, I felt the warm glow of our wonderful weekend still enfolding us.

But the next evening a call came for me on the landlady's telephone. It was my sister Lois. "Marge, my job at the cannery fell through. I need a place to live in Berkeley for a couple of weeks before my next job begins. Could I come and stay with you?"

I couldn't refuse. My bedroom did have an extra bed. "Oh, sure," I said in a welcoming tone I didn't wholly feel.

Nodding my thanks to the landlady, I left her parlor and walked back to the kitchen where Herb was making muffins for supper. When I told him about the new development, he surprised me by saying enthusiastically, "I'm heartily in favor of it."

His eagerness dismayed me. It suggested that he didn't cherish our private meals and talks as much as I did. I wrote in my diary,

> I know he likes her...and I want him for myself. Jealousy! Selfish! ...
> But if we're really meant to fall in love, it will happen anyway, despite
> her being here.... It'll be O.K.

For twelve days, three of us shared meals and discussions. Lois and Herb both indulged in ceaseless punning, banter, and bright cracks. I couldn't help getting involved, but I didn't enjoy it. I had tolerated the silliness at Fairfax as simply part of Herb's getting acquainted with my family, but this was too much.

More important, Herb seemed to be just as affectionate to Lois as to me. A cold fear crept into my heart. Maybe I didn't mean half as much to him as I fancied! Maybe he would fall for her instead of for me!

Friday evening the three of us went to the movies. Herb sat in the middle. My heart sang as he held my hand and squeezed it meaningfully. But when I shyly confessed this to Lois as we undressed for bed, she said he had held her hand too! She gave me sisterly advice about not jumping to conclusions. "He likes all of us girls," she said.

I tried to be decent to my well-meaning sister. When she suggested helpfully, at the breakfast table a few days later, "You ought to get a permanent wave in your hair, Marge," I restrained the protest I had made for years, that it wasn't "natural."

And then Herb added, "Yes, why don't you?"

Well! If he liked the idea...maybe...

But times of discomfort continued to bewilder me. One evening when I had withdrawn to take a bath, I could hear Herb and Lois talking and laughing in the empty dining room. I told myself resolutely, "I must not cling this way. Let happen what may, my main task is becoming aware of the mystery of being alive, and building peace in the world."

On Saturday, August 5, Lois left town for her new job, and to my great relief, Herb showed no signs of regret at her departure.

That afternoon I went to the beauty shop down on Center Street, and sat amazed while the operator wrapped my hair in small curlers, applied some kind of chemical, and attached the curlers by long wires to an electrical source. At long last she unplugged me, combed my locks, and held up the mirror. It looked frizzy to me, but Lois's always did too, right after a permanent, so I didn't worry about it.

I was grateful for a quiet dinner with Herb once more. He accepted my funny-looking hair and its funny smell without negative comment. But I thought he looked a little depressed.

"How did your organic chem turn out?" I inquired.

He shook his head grimly. "Oh, I flunked for sure. The final was impossible. I've certainly killed my chances of going any further in soil science." Then, all at once, he sat up straight on the kitchen chair and his face lit up. "But you know what? I feel kind of released and free. I'm in a mood to have some fun tonight. I'm not even going to think about tomorrow."

I was glad to see him out from under his cloud.

When the dishes were done, we left the house together. "Do we have any friends we could go see?" Herb asked, as we wandered up Bancroft toward Telegraph Avenue.

Golly, I didn't want to see anybody else! I just wanted a chance to talk with him alone. In fun, I suggested walking to Lake Merritt, some five miles away.

"Well, we could take the streetcar," he said.

We heard a rumble behind us, and Herb turned to look. "Here's one now! Come on!" And before I had time to think, he grabbed my hand and pulled me into the street to get on board.

All during that ride to Oakland we talked.

"What was your father like?" I asked.

"Mother always said he was a rascal. He had fine spiritual ideals, but he failed grossly in living up to them. He didn't work to support the family."

I thought of my Old Age clients. "You told me he was sixty-six when you were born. Was he too elderly to work? How was his health?"

"I remember he always had problems with his stomach," Herb acknowledged. "But I think there was more to it than that. He had two marriages before he met Mother, both unsuccessful. From what she told me, he wanted all the benefits and no responsibilities."

At 14th and Broadway Herb said impulsively, "Let's get off!" He escorted me swiftly to the door and down the car steps, and we mingled with the Saturday night crowds that thronged the sidewalk. When he put his arm around my shoulders, I readily put mine around his waist, and we ambled aimlessly down to 12th Street.

"Several blocks further this way is the Alameda County Charities Commission, where I work," I informed him. But it was not a safe area to explore on foot at night, so we turned around and started back the other direction. Holding hands, we drifted past closed stores and brightly-lit eating places and night spots toward 19th Street. We talked endlessly about our family backgrounds, a subject we'd become comfortable with.

Suddenly Herb staggered me with a direct, serious question. "What do you want, a career or a family?"

Family? Did he mean kids that he and I might have? This was pushing into more intimate territory than we had yet mentioned. My heart beat faster.

"I don't think the two are incompatible," I stammered. Inventing my simplistic philosophy as I went along, I continued glibly, "If you had the kids all in a bunch, they'd grow up and you'd still have time for a career yourself."

I found myself panting. "We've been going too fast," I said, slowing down. With linked arms we made our way along 19th Street to the grassy park at the edge of Lake Merritt, where we found an inviting bench.

The dark water lay still and beautiful with reflections from surrounding strings of lights. "This is a favorite spot from my childhood," I told Herb. "I grew up in Oakland, and we often came here for picnics and band concerts."

He pulled me close, apparently unconcerned that my hair reeked of ammonia. I settled my shoulders in the curve of his arm and laid my head against his cheek.

"What about Wim?" he asked gently. "I only know vaguely what happened."

I sketched the story for him, ending with, "It seems a long time ago, now."

He told me about his blighted romances with Elsie and Harriet. "Those seem a long time ago, too," he said.

Our talk stumbled on. "I think I've gotten over being young and foolish," Herb said. "I feel so strongly that you've got to have idealism as the basis for any intimate relationship, or it just doesn't work."

"Oh, yes! I agree."

"Then we can go on from there," he said firmly. "Some couples spend their whole lives adjusting to differences in their basic values."

Silently I jubilated, "Not us! Our basic values are amazingly in harmony." A deep sense of being completed filled my soul.

But one thing still puzzled me. My highest goal was to achieve a greater awareness of God. Could we move toward that goal together? I had sometimes considered the possibility that spiritual attainment might require a solitary, even hermit-like, devotion. I knew Herb had an assortment of esoteric philosophies in his background. I had to know how he leaned in this matter.

Awkwardly, but boldly, I asked my question. "Herb...do you think our joining forces...might be an obstacle to striving toward a higher consciousness?"

"An obstacle?" he repeated slowly. "No. I might have thought so a few years ago. But not now." He drew back to look straight into my eyes, smiled broadly, and gave the most beautiful answer I could have wished for. "No, I think two can do it!"

All at once the mountain of my uncertainty and caution crumbled and blew away. A great space lay open between us, where life and thought could flow freely from heart to heart.

Our faces came closer—and closer—till we were caught up in our first wonderful, tender kiss. We stopped for breath and kissed again.

Full of overflowing joy, we jumped up from the bench and shared a rapturous hug. The miracle had happened! We belonged together!

With wings on our feet, we raced across the park lawn, hand in hand, on our way to catch a streetcar for home. As we passed a policeman on his beat, I giggled, "He'll think we're running away with something."

Herb responded with a gleeful confirmation: "We are! We've found something nobody else has, haven't we!"

Our Impossible Dream
(1939)

Sunday morning I awakened to a new world. My bed was a fairy ship floating into dock from a sea of dreams. I had found my true love. My heart was ready to explore the wonderful land that stretched out before me. I rejoiced to name it "Herb and Margaret." Our separateness, I felt sure, was banished forever.

I shaved and dressed with care, wanting to present my best possible persona to Margaret. My one-and-only suit received a special brushing, and, of the three neckties I owned, I chose the red one to celebrate our lovers' hearts. I wanted to announce to everyone how happy I was, how special I felt.

Our Sunday breakfasts had always been later than on weekdays, and I timed my arrival at the kitchen door of my sweetheart's residence to fit her rising habits. When she turned the key, like powerful magnets we were pulled into each other's arms. Our flood of kisses transformed the drab kitchen into a royal palace. That lovely ruffled dress she wore became a queenly robe. Only the good sense, the practical sense, of my queen kept us anchored to the earth.

She whispered into my ear, "We've got to...stop this... and get breakfast...because ...I promised..."

When her words dwindled into silence, I whispered to her, "You promised what?"

She disengaged and smiled up at me with such adoration that I started all over again with our smooching, until she broke off decisively. "I promised Lois I'd do an errand for her, to return a book she borrowed from the Quaker Meeting House library." She stopped. "I mean, I thought it might be nice to attend the Friends Meeting for Worship this morning...unless you have some other plan."

I puzzled over this for a split second. "I thought you had a thing about not going to church."

"Quakers are different," she said. "I've only been to their silent worship twice before. I like them. They don't pretend to be something they're not."

I felt good about checking out such a piece of the new world I had entered. I had dressed for something special. Maybe this was it. We made our way through breakfast and walked the dozen blocks over to the north side of the campus to the corner of Walnut and Vine.

I gripped Margaret's hand firmly as we mounted the broad wooden steps, along with several other late arrivers. As we stepped through the doorway into the large worship room I was fascinated to see how starkly furnished it was with rows of folding chairs facing the fireplace. The simplicity appealed deeply to me.

Two things took possession of my inmost being during the hour that followed. First was the continuing amazement that I had found the love of my life, my soul mate. Second, I reveled in the peace and quiet that suffused the meeting. Here I found I could, with the encouragement of the Quaker community, enter into deeper meditation than I knew even in the solitude of my own room.

From time to time I opened my eyes to peek at Margaret by my side, and to know gratitude that a Power beyond myself had brought me into her life, and that she had been brought into mine, and that we would be together into the unknown, unfolding future.

At the end of the meeting we were greeted and welcomed by those near us. Margaret turned in Lois's borrowed book, and then we left to find our way home. We had everything to talk about. I shared my wonder about how the Spirit had brought us together against all odds. I confessed how blind I'd been not to see the "real Margaret" during all the months we'd been in the same co-op environment.

Berkeley was beautiful that day, garden greenery spreading down to our sidewalk, birdsong announcing our approach. As we walked along I couldn't contain the wonder that filled my soul. I simply had to spill over. On the corner of Walnut and Virginia I stopped abruptly and grabbed both hands of my sweetheart.

"Margaret! This thing that's happened to us is so BIG! It's like a door has been unlocked to endless power. I feel as though with you I can do anything!"

There was not the faintest hesitation in her response. "Oh, yes! Our love is too big for the power to be just for us. We have to give it to the world."

She kissed me right there in the midst of that warm noontime, on that Berkeley street corner, and I didn't care if the whole world saw it. I WANTED the whole world to see. We were in pursuit of a common dream, and that was all that mattered. Maybe we were going to be writers, maybe social workers, maybe counsellors, but for sure we would be helpers of people, one way or another.

Our dream was so important to us that we had not mentioned to each other the institution of marriage, nor even of engagement. I had not "proposed" to Margaret at Lake Merritt because in very recent months I had been twice rejected. I was perfectly happy to accept her suggestion that we "cross our fingers and see what happens." And yet by Wednesday I was ready for us to uncross our fingers.

Margaret's answer required patience of me. "Could we just be *engaged* to be engaged?" she asked, winsomely.

Toward the latter part of our first wonder-filled week, life called us to be "helpers of people" in a very mundane way, so ordinary that we scarcely noticed the connection with our dream. The girls of the eating co-op, now reduced to five, were trying to get reestablished at a new address and to recruit new members. They drafted us to help out with moving furniture, repositioning mattresses and doing miscellaneous repairs, which we did with a good will, while we kept our new relationship secret. We indulged in hugging and kissing only when we were alone.

On Saturday we gave them our whole day. While Margaret polished the bathroom mirror, I stood on a stool to adjust the overhead flushing tank that constantly leaked water into the bowl. When it was done I jumped down and impulsively pulled my beloved onto my lap as we sat on the closed toilet seat.

In that moment Mary paused at the open door. "Well!" she said. "What's going on? Are you two in love?"

We nodded ecstatically. I winked at Margaret. "In fact, you might even say we are engaged!" She nodded agreement, and we grinned blissfully at Mary.

For me that hour opened a door that had slammed shut when I failed organic chem. No longer could I postpone my career problem. I was soon to become a family man with primary responsibility to support a wife and children. I had to make some hard choices. I wanted a career that could embody the dream Margaret and I shared. In the secret place of my inner man I had played around vaguely with half a dozen options. Now the time had come for decision.

On the radiant Sunday afternoon that followed our uncrossing of the fingers, with chores done for the co-op, Margaret and I climbed the rickety ladder of an old water tower behind the house. It was the most private place we could find, taller than the co-op's second floor. We sat on the platform with legs dangling, and I laid out my thinking for inspection. I started by mentioning another couple that had found each other by eating at the co-op table.

"Mary and Marvin are talking about going to India as missionaries. That's one way of helping people in need. Marge, are you interested in that kind of work?"

She shook her head and reached for my hand. "That's good for them. Marvin was born in India. But it doesn't appeal to me."

"Yeah. Same here," I was quick to agree. "But I can see he's getting a lot out of his time at Pacific School of Religion. And so is Ricky...and Gene. What I've been playing around with..." I found it hard to come right out in the open with something so foreign to my experience.

"Yes?" Margaret looked up at me with a wry expression at the corner of her mouth.

"I mean...since it's helping people that you and I are interested in, I thought it might be a good idea to check out PSR...just to see what they have to offer. I mean...no strings attached. It might lead to useful training."

She was slow to respond. "Uh-huh."

I realized there was still a lot I didn't know about my companion. "But what do you think?"

"What kind of a job are you imagining?" she asked.

"Well, gee, I don't know. There's YMCA work. And there's college level teaching. And counselling. And religious education, like your dad's work... and of course, the ministry."

"Are you thinking seriously about the ministry?"

"Not really. Your dad's the only one I ever talked to." I became urgent, hoping for some note of confirmation. "At least I could go up to the school and ask questions."

She smiled faintly. "If it's something you really want to do, why don't you go ahead?"

When we climbed down off the water tower I felt a strange emptiness. I couldn't understand Margaret's lukewarmness, so sharply in contrast to everything else we had shared. Was she so involved in her own job that she couldn't pay attention to my need to explore new careers? Or maybe it was still her negative feelings about the church.

On the clearest of Monday mornings, with Margaret off to work, the urge to explore new options burned bright again. I made my pilgrimage to "holy hill," where PSR sat in splendid dominance one block north of the Cal campus. The gray stone administration wing of the school displayed a tiny sign: OFFICE. I climbed the stairs and greeted the lone secretary, who promptly ushered me into the inner sanctum of seminary president, Arthur Cushman McGiffert, Jr.

I found him exuding a gruff charm, not the polish of an academic executive. He was rather like Margaret's father. He was wiry, a small-sized athlete, one who enjoyed his physical life and at the same time a broad range of intellectual pursuits. What I didn't discover till later was that this was McGiffert's first day as the new president. He had been called from Chicago Theological Seminary to rescue the school from having to close its doors. During the Depression doldrums, the administration had run through all their endowment capital and desperately needed money to pay salaries. I was his first student, face to face, a symbol, the flesh and blood of a student body that was to come.

He wanted to know all about me, and I was prepared to tell all, but I didn't have to for his time was limited. His questions narrowed to a sharp focus.

"Herb, what is your motive for knocking on our door?"

I told him of my dissatisfaction with a career in soil science and that I really wanted to serve humanity, to help end war in the world, to ease suffering. I rode along gingerly on the very sketchy knowledge I had picked up about church programs of mercy. I couldn't guess whether I was anywhere near meeting the expectations of the school, but he nodded agreeably.

I raced ahead with the story of my teaching assistant job and the excitement of helping the students, and then the fact that I was engaged to be married.

"Oh? And who is the girl?"

"Margaret Waddell. Her father was professor of religious education here a couple of years ago."

"Congratulations! Yes. I know the name. And have you set a date for your marriage?"

"Not yet."

"That's good."

I didn't know what he intended by that. But I sensed that my linkage with a Preacher's Kid and association with her stable minister's family counted big as brownie points toward any possible admission to the school. I felt dutybound to expose more of my background.

"My childhood family rarely went to church," I said. What I didn't tell him was my mother's dream at my birth that I was destined to be a "world teacher." I felt that would seriously muddy up my prospects.

McGiffert surprised me with a brisk nodding of his head that virtually ignored my lack of church experience. He pressed harder on his central question. "And what do you think we at the school can do for you?"

"Well, I feel the church may have something to offer for solving the world's desperate problems, and maybe this school is the place to find out." His big smile encouraged me, and I plunged on. "I don't know if I'm cut out for the ministry particularly, but I'd like to try PSR as an experiment."

"Excellent," he said. "The next step, then, is to get some paperwork started." He buzzed for his secretary who served as registrar. "Bea, we have our first student. How do we do it?"

I was flabbergasted. The suddenness of the decision left me breathless. What had happened? When I had climbed the school stairs at ten a.m., I certainly had not made up my mind to become a seminary student. McGiffert hadn't tried to sell me on the school. Something larger than my will had been at work under the surface. I had enrolled in a Christian school for the training of ministers, I who had attended church only four or five times in my life.

When I walked down the stairs and paused for a look at San Francisco Bay, my excitement exploded. Vistas I never dreamed of swept across the sky, future worlds to explore, new people to meet, great adventures to dare. I didn't know how I could contain myself until five-thirty, when I would meet Margaret at her streetcar stop.

When the time came, though, I had simmered down a lot, enough to keep my feet on the sidewalk at the corner of Shattuck and Bancroft. I gave her my biggest hug and spilled out the tale of my morning. "Y' know, I went and registered. Classes start in a week," I exulted. "And McGiffert said I could have a partial scholarship job, working in the school library."

If Margaret was shaken by the suddenness of my decision to enroll, she didn't show it. All she said was, "So you've really decided to do it." She was amiable but seemed to imply it was my decision alone. I yearned to have it be our decision, a partnership commitment.

I fumbled in search of solid ground. "Funny part in the registration, they asked for my denomination. For a minute I thought I should write in Quaker. But they don't have ministers. So I told them Congregational. Like you."

Margaret wrinkled her nose at me. "But I'm not an active Congregationalist, you know. I dropped out."

We had not budged from our curbside rendezvous, and I made one more pitch. "But will you go along with this—as an experiment?"

She put an affectionate hand on my shoulder. "If it's what you really want to try, of course I'll go along." Her answer was not quite what I wanted, but for the moment it was the best I could negotiate.

As the evening traffic roared by on Shattuck Avenue and we headed for Margaret's place, the tumult of my inner life sped ever faster. So much! So much! Falling in love, engagement, change of career, new worlds to conquer! I squeezed her hand.

"Do you know who'll be happiest about our news?"

"Who?"

"My Mom! She wrote how she liked you." And then I added, "I think she'll be pleased about PSR too. It may even fit in with her world teacher dream. But that stuff always makes me feel uneasy."

Margaret threw me a troubled glance and did not pursue the peculiar birth-dream theme that haunted me.

"I've been thinking," I said, "Maybe I should catch the train for L.A. This is too big for a letter."

I did go to Los Angeles the very next day, and arrived late at the ramshackle, rented garden cottage that had been home to me a year ago. I kept tight rein on my news till after supper with Mother and Don, and then, still facing all the supper clutter on the table, I was ready for my moment of truth.

"Well, what's up, Bert?" That's what Mother always called me.

"I'm getting married to Margaret Waddell!"

Their response of silence fitted the shock I saw on their faces. Don broke the ice in his inimitable style.

"Hah! So we're going to have a married man in the family. When do we get to meet her?"

Mother added, "A very nice girl, Don. I've talked with her."

I jumped in with the rest of my news. "And that's only the half of it. I've enrolled for the fall term at Pacific School of Religion."

Mother looked puzzled. "Pacific School of Religion? What's that?"

"A theological seminary, for training ministers."

Don's reaction was blunt disbelief. "You, a minister?"

"Well, maybe. It could lead to YMCA work, or teaching, or other stuff." Somehow Margaret and our marriage got buried under the avalanche of their feelings about PSR.

Mother turned up the decibels of her anxiety. "If they knew about your background, the people of the church would never accept you."

"What do you mean? I don't get it."

"At the time you were born your father and I were not legally married. I told you that a long time ago."

"Well, they won't know," I declared. "And anyway times have changed." I couldn't feel any problem, except to wonder if Mother was still feeling guilty over her past.

Her mood grew more intense. "And what about soil science? You were headed for a good-paying job. You know how we barely scrape by. Ministry in the church is a poverty profession!"

I had to recite for her the unhappy details of my academic failure and of my disillusionment with any career in science. Then I plunged ahead with the dream Margaret and I had begun to shape, how we wanted most of all to serve humanity.

"Margaret's a wonderful girl," Mother declared emphatically, "the brightest of all your 'sisters' that came to visit. But I never thought she would turn you aside from a really practical career."

I was stunned. "She didn't turn me aside! It was my idea!" And then I reached far out beyond where my dream had yet taken me. "We're going to be healing the spiritual life of mankind. The sort of thing you have always said was of first importance."

"Don't you care anything at all for your family?"

That was the heart of her bitter complaint. Even though she had always preached about love for ones fellow humans, I realized again with guilty uneasiness, the bottom line was dollars and cents. She nourished a hope that, at last, I would be able to rescue her from a lifetime of penny-pinching.

But there was no way I would back off from my plan and goal, and there was no way I could see the possibility of getting Mother to come on board. "I'm sorry you feel that way," I said. "I thought you would be happy for me. I have to go ahead, regardless. I'm going to start PSR, and I'm going to marry Margaret."

I caught a warning flash in Don's eyes that said, "We're going to have big trouble from Mom." My soul was in deep pain. My declaration of independence had now moved us into open warfare.

I grabbed the train the next day, and mourned as I listened to coach wheels clicking along the rail. A strange hardness filled my heart, such as I had never known before. It seemed as though I had torn myself loose from the certainties on which my life had been built. I yearned to get back to my sweetheart, to pour out my woe.

In the late afternoon I met Margaret at her trolley terminal, and with arms entwined, we walked onto the campus toward the Campanile. I needed the extra support which the beauty of the trees and lawns would give. The burden I poured out to my mate-to-be was the heaviest. She responded with deep sympathy.

"But I thought," she said, "that you and your mother were very harmonious."

"Yeah. She always spoke of the 'special tie' between us, but I never knew what she meant by that. Maybe it had something to do with her 'world teacher' vision. All I knew was she was my mother, and I loved her. But this time I saw that our 'tie' was too strong to be healthy. I had to break the apron strings and stand on my own feet."

"Good for you," said Margaret. "I'm sure it will all work out. She'll get used to it."

We found a wooden bench in front of the Campanile, and gradually my anxieties ebbed. Margaret put an arm around my waist and laid her head on my shoulder. "I'm so glad you're back," she murmured. "I really missed you while you were gone."

We pressed our lips in a passionate kiss and I whispered my adoration. "You're the one I have a 'special tie' with now, Marge. I feel as though I have been looking for you for a million years."

"That's how I feel about you, too. Oh, Herb, I never thought there could *be* anyone like you. You're an inspiration."

Suddenly all of my heart hunger came welling up, driving me to share a wonderful idea that had been simmering just below the surface. I stood and pulled Margaret up to face me. "Marge!"

"Yes?"

"Let's get married right away! Next week!" I had half expected the shock I saw in her face, so I pressed on. "Why not? Let's start our married life and my new training all at once!" I was breathing heavily now, determined to persuade my darling. "So we won't have to live far apart, and so the inspiration won't fade away! The time is ripe!"

But now her whole demeanor changed from shock to terrible anguish. "Oh, no, not yet! Everything is happening so fast! It doesn't make sense. We should let things float for a while."

If she had slapped me in the face, her response could not have been more violent. I had been feeling that if I didn't start school and marriage at the same time, it might be a long time before we could marry. The trial balloon I had launched was punctured, dead, and something inside me withered.

I walked her home to her room and told her I didn't feel like eating supper. And the next morning I didn't show up for breakfast. I had all day to struggle with reality. This was an all-out quarrel, the first we'd ever had.

As I wandered aimlessly on campus pathways, fear gripped me that maybe the great dream we were building together would be impossible. Were we not on the same path? Could we not agree? The stakes were incredibly high. I had jumped ship from my mother and I needed a lifeboat to cling to. I needed this new woman who held my heart in her hands. I needed her immediately, to fill the empty place in my life. I couldn't wait. I needed her to give me security, now, and she had said, "No!"

Finally I began to realize there was an important difference in our personalities. Margaret's habit of decision-making was slow and logical and painstaking. Mine was fast and inspirational and impulsive. Here, for sure, was a reality I would have to come to terms with. But there was more.

A long forgotten image came seeping into my thoughts. The picture was that of my nursery crib, the earliest possible memory. I must have been only two or three years old. I watched along a darkened hallway out to a lighted parlor where my mother and my father shouted angry words. I did not understand what they were saying, but I feared they would hurt each other. In my terror I almost stopped my breathing.

At any rate, I knew deep in my soul that so long as the violence between my parents continued to shadow my subconscious I could never let myself quarrel with Margaret. Never again.

I met her trolley at the corner of Bancroft and Shattuck with a cheerful smile and a loving embrace. "I've been doing a lot of thinking today," I said. "You were right. We should wait."

Wedding March to a Different Drummer (1939)

Once Herb had agreed to wait, an infinite peace filled my being. Our storm of disagreement about getting married "next week" had shaken me up severely. I hadn't meant to make him suffer! I just gave him my honest reaction. When I saw how disappointed and sad he was, I felt terrible for hurting him. Yet I could not change my stand.

But now all was well again. I wrote in my diary,

> I feel happy and triumphant, because I know we'll solve any future difficulties this same way: remain steadfast and loving, and our wills will come into harmony.

Our reconciliation made it possible to talk peacefully about our coming wedding. "Maybe we can get married in Christmas vacation," I suggested dreamily the next evening, as we leaned against the railing of a footbridge over Strawberry Creek.

Herb perked up at my mention of a specific date. "That sounds good to me!" Swiftly he reached ahead with further ideas. "Our wedding won't be conventional, will it!" he declared.

I looked up in surprise, for I hadn't really thought of the details at all. "How do you mean?"

"We don't want ushers and bridesmaids and all that," he elaborated. "Like a big show to impress people."

His answer fitted perfectly with my mood of distancing myself from what I saw as empty rituals, like church services. "You're right," I said eagerly. "Who needs a long white dress and a three-tiered cake? Our wedding will be simple."

We looked at each other adoringly, as crickets in the dusk chirped their approval.

But we had a shock coming. In the PSR office a couple of days later, Herb mentioned to President McGiffert that we were thinking of having our wedding during Christmas vacation. McGiffert disapproved!

"He came on real strong," Herb told me at our kitchen table that night, as he broke the skin on his baked yam. "He said PSR's academic standards are high, and building a marriage would take time away from studies." He paused to take a mouthful.

I waited to hear more, as I thought privately that McGiffert didn't realize how much we were married in spirit already.

Herb poured milk into his glass and went on. "Then McGiffert asked, what if we had a baby?"

I protested, "But we don't intend to send for a baby right away!"

"That's what I told him. But he said accidents do happen, and it would complicate our lives drastically."

I fluffed that off. There would be no accidents; we knew all about contraceptives, from the pamphlets we had been reading, and we would be very careful. Finally I asked, "Well, how long does McGiffert think...?"

"He wants us to postpone marriage for three years—till I graduate from PSR. He says that's the way it is with all the other students."

"Three years!" I exclaimed. "That's ridiculous! Of course we won't wait that long!"

Herb's face brightened at my bold assertion. "I was afraid you might side with the administration," he confessed sheepishly.

"No," I chuckled, "I don't take their position very seriously." I plunged my spoon into the applesauce. "You've said this whole thing is an experiment," I reminded him. "McGiffert knows that, doesn't he? Why, you might not even *be* here for three years. All that part of our future is uncertain. The one thing we *are* certain about is that we're going to get married."

"That's for sure," Herb agreed, pounding the table with his fist.

As we washed the dishes, he had one more comment to make. "McGiffert can't *force* us to postpone marriage. He's just strongly *urging* us. But—" he stopped to shake suds from a plate, "he's shown a real fatherly concern toward me, taking me in and getting me oriented and all. I can't help feeling kind of sad that I have to go against him."

We soon found that Herb's swift leap into seminary brought unexpected requirements. When he next met me at my streetcar stop, he reported that he had to have a "field work" assignment.

"They want me to look into a position at a church in the Mission District in San Francisco. The pastor there is the Rev. Dillon Throckmorton."

"Throcky!" I exclaimed. "He's great! I've heard him speak at youth conferences. Do you know what you would be expected to do?"

"Not yet. I'm to go see him tomorrow."

The next evening at supper, my sweetie told me he was to be "Boys' Worker" at Throcky's church. It would mean leading a Boys' Club twice a week and a Sunday School class on Sunday mornings. He seemed a bit overwhelmed.

"I've never worked with young boys before," he said. "I never even belonged to Scouts or any kind of club."

"I'm sure you'll do fine," I said, with my unlimited faith in Herb's abilities.

He didn't seem quite so sure. "But there is one good thing about the job. I'll be paid $20 a month." He hesitated, and looked at me questioningly. "Throcky wants you to teach a Sunday School class of girls, too."

It had not occurred to me that I would be involved in Herb's field work. His obligations at PSR were his responsibility, not mine. But I couldn't let him down.

"I'll probably be going to San Francisco with you on Sunday mornings anyway," I said, "so I guess I might as well try the teaching."

When he met my streetcar a few days later, he had news that would affect our daily lives on another front.

"I'll be moving into the PSR dorm on Sunday," he said cheerfully. "If you could find a place to live close by, you could come up and have breakfasts and dinners with me in the Benton Hall dining room. I've cleared it with the kitchen staff."

Even though that would pull me further into the PSR institution, I was delighted with the prospect of continuing to have meals with my beloved, and started hunting the next day. On Saturday afternoon I found a cute little backyard "hut" on Walnut Street. Ten feet square, it was set behind a large house, and its brown weathered exterior suggested it had once been a storage shed. It had been remodeled into a rustic bedroom. The low ceiling, flowered curtains, tiny wood stove for heating, along with a porcelain basin and pitcher for washing, appealed to my storybook romanticism.

I took Herb to see it. "I have the use of the bathroom in the big house," I explained. "I can keep bread and peanut butter and stuff on the shelf here to make my lunches. And the rent is only $7.50 a month!" He clapped his hands approvingly.

Suddenly we were hit by something far more important than our pleasant new living arrangements.

We had not been unaware of the danger in Europe. We knew Hitler had taken over Austria, then Czechoslovakia, and was poised to enter Poland. In spite of all that, I kept clinging to a thin thread of hope that a wider war could be averted. The first week of September, the thread broke. Big black newspaper headlines that I read on street corners shrieked, "Hitler marches into Poland." A day or two later, "Britain and France declare war against Germany."

There was no television in those days to bring us actual pictures of the events. Herb and I rarely saw the newsreels in movie theaters, but what we heard on the radio in Benton Hall was frightening enough. Reporters spurted out the news in rapid-fire emergency style, and spoke of the nervous and jittery mood of the American public.

I felt sick about the war. For years I had been a passionate peacemaker. When I was fourteen, I was shocked by books and films about the conflict of 1914-18 that revealed the horrors of war. Sunday School and church nurtured my devotion to Jesus' teachings about brotherhood, love and forgiveness—the exact opposite of war. When I rebelled against the church in college days, it was partly because it seemed to me most church members failed to challenge the whole war system.

By the time I was twenty, I worked faithfully in the "peace movement" on the campus and in the community. I believed that by giving speeches and passing out leaflets, I was really helping to change people's minds. If enough of us wrote letters to Congress, I thought, our representatives would change American policies and have a good effect on the world.

But all my efforts had been in vain. The unthinkable tragedy had come. I was not sure, any more, that even the limited peace slogan, "Keep America Out of War," was realistic.

The night Herb and I took our first turn at dishwashing duty in the steamy Benton Hall kitchen, the small radio on the counter blared forth intense news of the accelerating violence: "Nazi forces are bombing Warsaw, Poland's capital. The populace is in panic."

Herb and I looked at each other in shared pain, and as soon as our chores were finished, we escaped into the cool air outdoors. I slipped my hand into his as we walked along one of the concrete pathways that crisscrossed the lawns between the PSR buildings. We stopped at the western exit from the campus, and looked across a misty San Francisco Bay to where a deep orange sun was making its farewell decline.

"Sunsets are so beautiful, and war is so hideous," I sighed. "How can they both be in the same world?"

Herb was quiet for a few moments, and then observed, "I've never been the peace activist that you have. But in my heart I've always longed for a world at peace. War never really solves anything, and it hurts everybody."

A bank of gray fog swallowed the red sun, and the air grew colder. I buttoned my sweater, Herb pulled his brown felt hat close, and we descended the cement stairs to Arch Street to begin our customary evening ramble. As we turned onto Virginia Street, we passed the lighted windows of quiet homes where families dwelt in peace.

A thought came to me that I could not avoid speaking. "Herb, if we should get into the war, and there's a draft, would you refuse to go? Be a conscientious objector?"

"Probably. I certainly wouldn't pull the trigger—on anybody."

"You might have to face prison. Many C. O.'s went to prison in the last war."

"Don't think I haven't considered that," Herb said slowly. "I hope I'd be strong enough to follow my conscience."

"We might have to be separated!" I said with a pang of fear. But I was glad of his stand.

Darkness had fallen. Householders drew their blinds, and we had only an occasional porch light to guide our steps. At Cedar and Walnut Streets, we found ourselves at the North Congregational Church. We gravitated to the side entrance, where we had sat on the steps once before, and snuggled close against the chill of the gathering fog.

"I feel so helpless," I lamented. "There's nothing we can do to stop the avalanche. It's too big for us."

Herb joined my lament. "Yeh. We're just two little nobodies, here on the church steps, half a planet away from the madness that's driving Europe...and the world...toward...toward the abyss."

The one thing we could do, we did. We clung to that fragment of goodness we knew best, the warm love that had filled our small personal world with tenderness and joy.

As we wrapped our arms tightly around each other, Herb whispered, "If two people can care for each other the way we do, then the human race can't be totally without hope!"

A few nights later, reluctant to part, we lingered outside my hut, while the brilliant, haunting music of Cesar Franck's *Symphony in D Minor* flowed over us from a neighbor's radio.

"I wish I didn't have to leave you and go back to the dorm every night," Herb said longingly.

On impulse I suggested, "Maybe we should move our wedding up to Thanksgiving."

As it turned out, we soon moved it closer than that!

My mother wrote that my Oakland cousin, Virginia, and her fiance Charlie, had set their wedding date for Saturday October 14. My folks would be coming north from Los Angeles for that occasion.

When I passed the news on to Herb at the PSR breakfast table the next morning, suddenly a thought struck me. "Hey! Why not have our wedding on the next day, October 15, and save the folks a second trip?!"

Herb was most enthusiastic. "Of course!" His discomfort over bucking the administration had eased since word had spread among the students that the uncertainties of war had changed the faculty's position on student marriages.

Did neither of us see the irony that I, who had protested a late August date as "too soon," now led the way in proposing a date in mid-October? The utter foolishness of getting married in the middle of Herb's school term did not enter our thoughts at all.

I sent a letter to my mother, barely a month before the nuptial date, telling of our decision. My innocent concluding sentence was,

Just a matter of cooking up a little ceremony and we'll be all fixed.

It sounded simple. But pressure from my family and relatives soon involved us in much, much more.

First of all, Auntie Helen and Auntie Laura arranged a bridal shower for both Virginia and me. I hadn't even thought of such a possibility! When I arrived on the front porch of Auntie Helen's modest house in East Oakland, Auntie Helen herself opened the door. Her abundant black hair, pinned in swirls and puffs on top of her head, fascinated me as always. She greeted me with her usual exuberance, and I thought I saw a special twinkle in her eyes. When Herb had phoned her for my address on that fateful July 9, had she guessed or foreseen that he would be the love of my life?

I sat down among the bright-eyed aunts and cousins who filled the small parlor and spilled over into the dining room. Being an object of their attention brought a kind of pleasure, but as Virginia and I opened the gifts of shiny new housekeeping articles and dainty nightgowns, I had mixed feelings. These material possessions would be useful; yet how far short they fell of touching the essence of our wedding: our deepening love for each other!

My parents, far from being stunned as they were when we had surprised them in August with our sudden engagement, received our decision for the October 15 date quite calmly. Mother couldn't wait to participate in the planning. She deluged me with questions:

Why don't you tell us what your plans are about refreshments? Do you want me to make a dark fruit cake from the family recipe that has been handed down? Where do you think of being married? And where do you plan to live?

In trying to answer some of her questions in my next letter, I inadvertently ran into a hornet's nest. I wrote her that the place of our wedding depended on how many people came.

You see, we'd like to keep it under 25 if possible. So, we can't invite relatives wholesale. We'll have to do some careful selecting.

Mother was devastated! She wrote back,

You can't do "careful selecting" among relatives.... All of Daddy's relatives, and mine, would feel very much hurt if they aren't invited.... A wedding has certain "traditions" and "customs" that can't entirely be overlooked.

My first reaction was, "Oh, hell! Why must tradition come in and spoil what we are planning ourselves? We don't want a gala reception for a host of relatives!"

My father added his page of persuasion:

I endorse and emphasize all your mother has said. You and Herb are parts of a complex network of social relationships. You would not want to have any hurt feelings associated with your wedding as you look back on it....

Whatever you decide to do, we will of course cooperate, but we urge you to consider seriously our joint suggestions.

My sister Lois, now in her senior year, did her best to be a peacemaker. She suggested to Herb and me that we "must not be selfish."

Under all this onslaught, it took only a day or two for me to shift my attitude. "Maybe we have been inconsiderate," I said to Herb as we sat on the steps of the PSR library after dinner. "Maybe these relatives do have an interest and curiosity."

"But I don't know any of these people!" Herb complained. "I have only my mother and my brother and my uncle in Iowa. You have dozens of relatives."

"Well," I explained gently, "my mother was one of five children, and my father one of four. So all those, plus their spouses and children, do make up quite a bunch. And most of them live nearby—around Berkeley or Oakland."

"So you want us to invite them all?"

"I think so. You know," I reminded him archly, "we profess to love all of humanity."

He gave up. "O.K. Let's invite them." He made a wry face. "We always want to kick over tradition, but I see we do have to live with people who value it."

I was glad we had come to a meeting of minds. "Besides," I pointed out, "I'd like to show them what a wonderful man I got for a husband!"

My parents must have been relieved to get my letter of October 1. Besides agreeing to invite all the relatives, I informed them that the wedding would be in Benton Hall at PSR, at three o'clock, and exulted that we had paid a one-dollar deposit on a $25 apartment we had found. We gloried in being unconventional as we wrote a hundred invitations by hand on penny postcards.

Gusts of tradition continued to buffet us, nevertheless. Our friends from the Grove Street co-op and from peace groups we belonged to held a kitchen shower for the two of us. A dozen PSR students brought us a welcome pile of canned goods—though, as a prank, they had torn off the labels! A huge package came in the mail from Auntie Helen: a set of really attractive everyday dishes! Cousin Virginia sent an electric iron. Gradually my skeptical attitude to such material things mellowed. I wrote to my mother, "Maybe presents are not such a bad idea after all!"

We still tried to be innovative in whatever ways we could. We originally thought of having our wedding rings made of bronze, with an infinity symbol on them. When Herb's research convinced us that bronze would stain our fingers green, we settled for plain gold wedding bands. The price for the two was $15, to be paid at the rate of two dollars a week.

Most important of all, Herb and I labored over plans for the wedding service itself. Although we had consented to a larger gathering, we were committed to making it express us. It would be unique.

Our student friends were eager to help. One volunteered to bring his phonograph, others would lend records of our favorite classical music, including Schubert's *Unfinished Symphony*. Nine of them agreed to join Herb and me in a "chorus," to sing a few favorite hymns for the guests.

On an evening about a week before the wedding, Herb and I sat at the round dining table in our newly-rented apartment, where Herb had already taken up residence, reviewing all these arrangements. I reported on my father's last letter.

"He agreed to be the official clergyman," I said, "and he wants to give a short talk around the symbolism of the Unfinished Symphony. Something about marriage being a thing of harmony, and it's unfinished because it keeps on going."

"I guess that'll be O.K.," Herb replied. "I hope he doesn't make it too long. We were planning for you and me to do most of the talking, weren't we?"

"Oh, we will."

On my way home from work a day or two later, I made a quick stop at Capwell's department store. I picked out a light blue, satiny dress, sprinkled with small navy-blue polka dots, for my wedding garb. It cost all of $4.00, but I figured I could use it also for Sunday best in the months to follow. It didn't quite fit, but I thought I could fix it. Fortunately, I had help—from Herb's mother! Arriving in Berkeley a few days before the wedding, she was careful to avoid any controversy with Herb. When she offered to alter my dress at the waist and sleeves, I accepted gratefully.

Saturday night, October 14, we didn't make it to Virginia's wedding. We were at our round dining table still putting finishing touches on our own ceremony. Herb got out his clunky old Underwood, and I typed the final order of service, and the several speeches we were to give. After blue-pencilling it with "stage directions," Herb walked me home to my hut, and we kissed a parting goodnight for the last time.

Why in the world would Herb and I go to San Francisco to teach Sunday School on the morning of our wedding day? But we did! We took our responsibilities at Grace Church seriously. But both of us spent the lesson time telling our classes the story of our romance!

On our way home, we walked past a florist shop on University Avenue. "Let's get a couple of flowers," I suggested. "One for my hair, and one for your buttonhole." The clerk offered us two yellow roses, and charged only five cents because they had broken off from their long stems.

At three o'clock, the stirring strains of *Beethoven's Fifth Symphony* on the phonograph welcomed the company that gathered in the transformed dining room of Benton Hall. Rows of steel folding chairs replaced the long tables at which Herb and I had eaten so many meals. The guests sat down quietly, facing a west window, not knowing quite what to expect. The only "decoration" meeting their eyes was a large basket of flowers, contributed by Auntie Laura, resting on a table in front of the window.

When the music of Beethoven ended, our chorus clustered around the piano and sang with heartfelt vigor while our dear friend Mary accompanied with skill and verve.

Herb and I then took chairs in front of the basket of flowers, facing the audience. They may have been been bewildered that we just sat there in silence, but soon caught on that they were to do likewise, during the first movement of the *Unfinished Symphony*. As we looked over the sea of faces, we picked out our immediate families, and, yes, a good many of my relatives, but also friends from eating co-ops, peace groups, and seminary—even several of the PSR faculty. I felt good that this whole community was celebrating with us.

When the music stopped, my groom and I stood up with our scripts in hand, a brash, starry-eyed couple, naively confident.

After Herb's formal, friendly greeting and my rather verbose introductory remarks, we signaled my minister father to leave his seat in the audience and present his sermonette. Then Herb and I took turns telling of our joy in finding each other, and of our hope for "higher and higher spiritual marriages that reach toward an inexpressible union."

In a simple ritual of our own creating, we picked up rings from the table behind us, and I began. "As a symbol of our unity, I, Marge, place this ring upon your finger, Herb. Let it bear witness to the world that you are my husband." Herb spoke similar words to me, and we kissed demurely.

My father, after reading a beautiful classic prayer "For All True Lovers," made a statement equivalent to "pronouncing us husband and wife," but not using those words. What he said was, "True marriage is not dependent upon formal pronouncements because it is an experience of the soul," and then, "We anticipate for these two young people a married life that shall be in very truth an 'Unfinished Symphony'—forever eager, forever joyous, and forever young."

Herb and I next spoke our "vows of dedication." Herb began,

> O God! We stand before you, before your world of nature, before society. We feel our love for each other shot through with a divine power, and we know that the joy we have been permitted has been through your guidance.

I followed with,

> But our love is too great to be bound up within ourselves. It would reach out to others.

We went on to describe, alternately, some of those others calling to us: the neglected old man with trembling hands on the park bench; the young boy exposed to the ways of crime in the filth of the city; the broken-spirited woman slaving in fields and orchards; bewildered families in war-torn countries.

Herb closed with a prayer:

> Help us, O God! Keep us ever alert to find the paths you have opened up for us, that we may answer these calls most truly.

In unison, we promised earnestly, "To this end we consecrate our lives."

At the conclusion, just after the Campanile on the University campus struck 4:00, we had all the guests come up and sign the back of our marriage certificate, while Wagner's *Overture to Die Meistersinger* rolled triumphantly from the phonograph.

Handshakes and congratulations followed, and a few snapshots. The guests enjoyed fruit punch and cupcakes, which my mother had devotedly prepared. She had laid aside her own desires to make a "dark fruit cake," and lovingly cooperated in our simpler style.

For Herb, only one cloud shadowed our radiant happiness: President McGiffert had not attended the celebration. Herb felt sure it was because he was still critical of our defying the standard he had set. But even that was softened—Mrs. McGiffert came!

Honeymoon Cottage
(1939)

American society of the twentieth century did the best it could for me on October 15, 1939. Without any doubt, marriage to Margaret was my "rite of passage." Custom had laid out the path: courtship, engagement, wedding, and finally, the honeymoon. Follow these steps, Herb, and you will pass from adolescence into adulthood, and be prepared, as a married man, to develop your own family.

Wonderful! Except that Margaret and I were deep into challenging all sorts of social traditions, eager to blaze our own trail. We felt the world was not as it should be, and we wanted to make whatever improvement we could. Our marriage, of course, would be a big opportunity to show a better way.

Our friends had the last word in the final ritual of our wedding. On the PSR lawn they showered us with conventional rice. When it was over I grabbed Margaret's hand, and we set out on an unconventional walk of six blocks that would take us to our honeymoon cottage.

We came to the porch of our separate garden entrance, a charming first-floor tack-on to the big house known as the Rose Lawn Apartments. I didn't sweep bride Margaret into my arms to cross the threshold; hand in hand we took possession of our new home. We thought of it as a "cottage" even though the rooms were bound tightly to the main two-story house. The honeymoon cottage included one compact living room plus a modest dining room, a kitchenette, bathroom, and a sunporch-bedroom. We stood in silent delight, alone for the first time as a married couple.

That's when I swept her into my embrace. "Marge, Marge, Marge," I whispered into her wavy brown hair. In the middle of our new home we kissed our way into ecstasy. A secret monologue echoed through my head. "I'm a married man! I'm a husband! This is my wife!"

Our first responsibility crowded urgently into our thoughts. Foolishly we had insisted on serving a "wedding supper" for our immediate families: my mother and brother, and Margaret's father and mother and two sisters. We wanted to show them our new home, and, also, we were uncomfortable about putting any additional financial burden on anyone. We hustled, for they would knock at our door within the hour. Margaret began cutting up string beans while I set the table with our new dishes and silverware.

And then they arrived, all of them together. I heard their voices as they came onto the porch, and as I ran to the door I nearly tripped on the ragged hole that made our aged carpet a booby-trap. It was the one thing in our lovely nest that irked me, and which I wanted to hide from our guests' eyes.

Mother was quick to comment. "What's the matter with the carpet?"

I responded defensively. "The landlady hasn't got around to buying our new rug yet. She promised, but..." And then I cut off apologizing and escaped into conversation with Ralph. None of the rest of the family indulged in comments that would make me feel self-conscious.

Margaret's sisters continued to replay the experience of the wedding ceremony as we all sat down to supper. They seemed pleased with our innovative effort. We ate together, and when it was over, our families departed promptly. Margaret and I heaved a sigh of relief. Alone at last.

Cautiously we tiptoed toward the unfamiliar waters of our sexuality. Curiosity and anxiety pulled me in opposite directions. Both of us were virgins and neither of us knew the protocol. It didn't help that Margaret looked to her new husband as one who knew what to do next. She assumed I was the thoroughly self-confident Man! I wasn't!

We moved by silent agreement, eyes smiling at each other, accepting our awkwardness; we stepped from our dining room down a single tread into the cozy sunporch glassed in on three sides. The westering sun filled our nest with romantic haze, which I reluctantly shut out as we closed the tall muslin drapes to insure our privacy. A lone bare light bulb glared down from the ceiling. For softening effect we lit a candle on the bedside stand, turned back the covers and then stood pantomiming our common "What next?" question to each other. For once we did not escape into philosophizing.

I began to unbutton my shirt. Margaret slipped off her blue wedding dress, and in less than a minute we stood naked before each other for the first time. I rejoiced in our natural bodies, excited that we had nothing to hide.

For me it was an awesome moment. The society I had grown up in forbade men to stare at an unclothed woman's body, except perhaps in a brothel. But here, in marriage, it was prescribed, accepted, expected. My eyes felt hot in my head; I found myself breathing fast and shallowly. Somewhere in the back of my mind I noted that Margaret was not playing coy. She just stood there waiting expectantly. I realized the next step was up to me. I took her into my arms, skin against skin, with a long, lingering kiss, and then I helped her onto the white sheets of our sprawling double bed.

That first night was a modest disaster. All of the best information I had about techniques and contraceptives I could probably have left in the library. I found our struggle to adapt to one another a hard run of frustrating trial and error. There were no words that would help, no guide book, no mentor. And no orgasm. After an hour we collapsed into each others arms, content to be patient. I wondered if sex was all it was cracked up to be. Margaret did not blame me for not having all the answers. In fact she seemed quite content just to fall asleep beside me.

Fortunately Margaret's boss at work insisted she take Monday off—perhaps wisely guessing that her productivity would be nil anyway. I was not so smart; I insisted on attending my first class of the week at three o'clock, an act of super-responsibility. The seminary had its hooks in me deeper than I had guessed.

Margaret went with me, and we basked in the smiles of fellow students. We also gathered clues that maybe some of them thought we were idiots to contaminate our honeymoon with academics. After the class we raced home to a candle-lit dinner and then at last to bed.

Maybe our first-night struggle had been necessary to clear away the rubbish of fear. Maybe our brains had been too busy.

"Shall we try again?" I proposed.

"I'm ready."

Margaret's easy acceptance of our human fumbling set me free. The mechanics of coupling seemed less distracting. We relaxed into each other. Gentle stirrings became stronger. We found a happy rhythm that awakened our wonderment.

And then the miracle happened. Nothing had prepared us for the exaltation that swept over us. A force larger than our separate selves took possession. Our bodies became the instrument of some wonderful symphony beyond our wildest imaginings. Our voices cried out in strident chorus, a shared agony of joy that took us where we had never been before. We ended the cycle transformed, panting, victorious.

What had happened to us? We had slipped across the frontier of creation, caught a glimpse of the abyss of heaven, and heard angels singing.

Truly, there are no words in any language that can make the moment live for anyone else. As we lay side by side we sang one of our favorites out of the Hollywood romantic tradition, "Ah, sweet mystery of life, at last I've found thee!" Not just bodies but spirits too. I nurtured a secret gladness that neither of us had sought out sexual partners before our marriage. This was too perfect to be shadowed by any experimental preludes.

The next morning, with sunshine seeping in through our curtains, we awoke in a golden glow, exulting over what, forever after, we would refer to as our "second night." Our gushing words came out of a common flood of feeling.

"You were wonderful!" I said to Margaret.

"You too!" she grinned. "You were so gentle and tender and patient—even on our first try the night before. And now look what happened!"

I caught my breath. "Aha! That must be one of the things we meant when we said, 'Two can do it.' Only we didn't know that sex would be a big part of our 'doing'."

I was ready to believe our final ego barriers had been leveled, and that we were no longer TWO but ONE. In our laziest of mornings I lay deliciously at peace and mused over what it would be like to live out our union through all the years to come, hand-in-hand in a thousand daily details.

Apart from that dreamy projection, of one thing I was very sure: God had given me more than just a woman to companion me—God had given me the gift of MARGARET, a unique and rare individual. The boyish co-ed I had known four months ago had completely vanished. Her body, designed with modest buxomness, sang of future promise—that one day she would bear and nurse our children.

Naive Expectations
(1939)

When Herb led me toward our bedroom on our wedding night, I had no idea what to expect. I trusted he would show me what to do. Didn't males have some inner knowledge about these things through instinct or dreams?

In my childhood, Mother told me how babies got started. I pictured the couple sitting on a rag rug in a cold bathroom, the man mechanically "placing" his seed into the woman's body, using his organ designed for that purpose. My reaction was, "Well, gosh, I'd sure have to love a man an awful lot to let him do such a thing as that!" I had no impression there were any pleasant feelings involved.

No sex education was included in the high school curriculum in those days, but over the years I read or heard that sex, when done as an expression of love, was a beautiful thing. When I was sixteen, I read a book in which intercourse was described as "the most intense, exquisite physical pleasure known to human beings." I couldn't imagine what that might be like.

During adolescence, any faint suggestion of sexual feelings "below my waist" caused me to run away from them or shut them down. I had somewhere picked up the notion that those things were "not pure," and it was wrong to dwell on them.

A few days before the wedding, I rode with my mother on the streetcar to see a doctor she wanted me to visit. On the way we had time to talk. Now that I was about to be a wife, like her, I made bold to ask a question I would previously have considered too private: "Do you wear pajamas or a nightgown for intercourse?"

She took my ignorant query in stride. "Well, dear, I don't wear anything. If I already have a nightgown on, I take it off." Oh! That was sure news to me.

From such a background I came to our first night. As Herb and I found our way, through patient experimenting, I was amazed and awed. On our second night, I felt the skies open to sweep us up to the heights together. I had never dreamed such sweetness was possible.

In the weeks that followed, we often had good times in our sexual coupling, even approaching our "second night" ecstasy. Some other times were less satisfying. But that didn't bother me much. For me, more important than physical union were our frequent feelings of intense closeness and tenderness, like "falling in love all over again." These were mountain peaks—"spiritual orgasm." I asked Herb one day, "Don't you think sex is really secondary to the waves of deep unity that sweep over us?" He seemed to agree, and I thought that was what we both believed.

In fact, I assumed we had common opinions on everything. We would need no "period of adjustment," such as newlyweds were supposed to go through, I thought arrogantly.

Then I found I was wrong! When we unpacked our clothes, to hang them on the bar in the parlor closet, Herb challenged the standard arrangement. "Why put all the man's garments at one end and the woman's at the other?" he said, with a pioneer's excited gleam in his eyes.

For a minute I was taken aback. But since I myself had always been ready to question many of the culture's accepted practices, I quickly adjusted my thinking to conform to his. "O.K.," I said. "Let's mix them up in no particular order."

That system proved inconvenient, of course, and convinced us both that we had to abandon it.

Herb startled me with another innovative suggestion a few nights later. We'd been playing borrowed records on a borrowed phonograph, and they lay scattered over the floor of our little parlor. Bedtime came, and I started to pick them up. "Let's just leave them there tonight," Herb urged. I hesitated. Yet because I was still intrigued by his novel ideas, I yielded. When one record got broken under a footstep, I began to see that my orderly habits might be more practical than his impulsive deviations.

We clashed more severely on an issue that was very important to me. I had a violin on long-term loan from a relative that had brought me much joy during college days. When I first plunged into marriage, I expected to have time to keep on playing it. One Sunday evening, therefore, I set up my music rack in the dining room. I got my violin out of its case, tightened the bow and rubbed rosin on the hairs, tuned the strings, and began to practice some exercises. Herb was sitting in the one easy chair in the parlor, reading, I supposed. After limbering up my fingers, I started in on a favorite piece of classical music.

Suddenly Herb let out a harsh protest. "Marge! Can't we do something *together*?"

I stopped, completely puzzled. We'd been doing things together all day! That afternoon we had sat in the parlor at the small drop-leaf table my parents had given us, writing thank-you notes for wedding presents on pretty blue note paper. Our work was lighted by a graceful ceramic lamp, also a gift from my folks, and I loved to hear the hourly chiming of the beautiful electric clock my colleagues at work had sent. I took it for granted that Herb had enjoyed our pleasant afternoon as much as I had. Why would he feel shut out now? And wasn't I ever to play my violin any more?

Finally, longing to repair the breach between us I said quietly, "I really have been hoping for a good chance to practice my fiddle again. This seemed the right time."

Herb could not see my reasoning. "I don't enjoy being a captive audience," he said morosely. "Can't we be a family?"

Reluctantly, I tried to compromise. "Well...just let me finish this one piece." I started pulling the bow over the strings again, but my left hand trembled as I tried to hold the instrument steady, and the bow, in my right hand, wobbled. All at once my precious violin slipped from my grasp and fell to the floor. I looked down in horror at the long crack in the sound box. Now I *couldn't* play any more!

Herb and I stared at each other in shared shock and guilt. All we could understand at the time was that we were both somehow off the track. I put my damaged fiddle away, and we found tearful comfort in each other's arms. We knew we had more "adjusting" to do.

Pressure from Herb's dominating mother also required adjustment from both of us.

I thought for awhile that she had become reconciled to Herb's independence. Before the wedding, she had written to me,

> I confess I was at first deeply disturbed to hear about Bert's change of plans for his life work. But the more I think about it, the more I realize that he will be happier and better suited to a path of life in which he is either teaching, or preaching, or ministering *directly* to humanity.... Perhaps there is a right place for him within the framework of the orthodox church.

The letter concluded:

> I joyously deliver my son into your care.... I want to have the grace and the wisdom to withdraw from my children's lives so that they may be truly free individuals.

She had been on her best behavior at the wedding, and I felt hopeful she would succeed in letting us be "free individuals."

But five weeks after the wedding, she came up from Los Angeles on the train for a visit of several days. We put her up on a couch in the dining room and tried to be friendly and courteous, yet she deluged us with criticisms and advice. Observing the flowered cushions I had created to make our second-hand wicker setee more like an upholstered sofa, she exclaimed with disgust,

"Why did you use such an ugly green fabric?" To her adult son, she gave advice she had no doubt nagged him with in the past: "You shouldn't tip your head forward like that when you look up with your eyes; it makes too much of the white show."

Most of all, she complained bitterly that we were shutting her out of our lives. She resented whatever time we spent on our employment obligations during her stay. When she inquired slyly whether we understood that there was an *art* to sex, our refusal to discuss the subject made her feel rejected. Time and again she scolded and accused, raged and wept.

After returning to Los Angeles, she wrote numerous letters to Herb, constantly harping on the "psychological estrangement" between them:

> I would like to feel a rich, beautiful mental and spiritual relationship between you and me, such as we have had.... Why can not such a tie exist, even tho' you are absorbed in Margaret and your marriage and your profession?

In his answering letters, Herb tried desperately to explain to her his struggle to become mature. He told her bluntly that, if he could throw off the feeling of being controlled by her "mothership," he could develop a real "friendship" with her. These replies never satisfied her. In our wedding service we had vowed to help humanity, but how to help Mother Dimock baffled us.

"When I was a little boy," he said one night as I sat on his lap after supper in our tiny kitchen, "I wrote a poem about a squirrel. Mother complimented me on it, and then proceeded to suggest a different word here, and a better phrase there, and a better rhyme in another place. It did improve the poem, but I grew to depend on her to be creative *for* me."

"But you are a creative person!" I declared, rubbing my cheek against his. "Look how cleverly you managed the pet show for your Boys' Club—so that every pet got some kind of award!"

"That's different from trying to think straight," Herb insisted. "The place I have the most trouble is writing papers for my classes. I'm beginning to see that it's because I have so often let Mom do all my thinking for me."

One night Herb's frustrations in drove him into an emotional crisis. He paced up and down in Honeymoon Cottage, very distraught. "I must be going insane!" he cried. "Something has got to snap soon!"

I was alarmed. "What is it, honey?"

"I've been working on this sermon for my preaching class for three weeks now, and I haven't got beyond the introduction. My mental machinery just won't work!" He covered his face with his hands.

I hurt for my beloved, but my lame words and gestures of sympathy failed to make any difference.

"I've tried to let go," he said, continuing his restless pacing. "I try to re-member 'it's Christ within who writes the sermon,' but there's some barrier I can't break with my will. Oh, I feel sick in my gut!"

Suddenly he swooped up his jacket and headed for the door. "I'm going to walk around the block," he called back over his shoulder.

His exit frightened me. I had never seen him so upset before. My heart beat faster, and horrible scenarios came to mind. Might he indeed crack up mentally? I felt torn to pieces.

Looking for something normal to focus on, I picked up my little clippers and concentrated on cutting my fingernails over the wastebasket near the front window. I mulled over some of the things Herb had passed on to me from his psychotherapy class under Dr. Fritz Kunkel. Suddenly I remembered his re-port about the function of a "crisis" in an individual's life. "A psychological crisis," Herb had told me, "means the egocentric shell is breaking. And that gives the person an opportunity to live more nearly from the true center, the Real Self."

I was glad for the idea that this painful confusion had a positive possibility. I prayed it would prove true for my dear one.

At last I had to recognize that I could do nothing to help Herb directly. In a leap of faith, I let go of my anxiety, and found peace in trusting that divine forces would bring him through the process of the crisis.

An hour later, I heard Herb coming up the front steps, and ran to open the door. I saw by his relaxed expression of face that he was subdued and feel-ing better. He came inside and held out his arms for an embrace. I had just been smearing vaseline on my chapped lips, and as we kissed, Herb got a smear of vaseline too! It struck us both funny, and sent us off into gales of laughter that brought healing release from the tensions of the evening.

By the following Sunday afternoon, Herb felt ready to tackle the unfin-ished sermon again. He spread out his papers on our dining table, and I sat nearby mending socks.

After awhile he looked up. "Midge."

"Yes?"

"Maybe you could help me on this."

"I can certainly try." I laid my mending aside and drew my chair closer to the table. "What's your message?" I asked. "What are you trying to say?"

He answered with a self-deprecatory smile, "My title is 'The Success of Failure."

"Intriguing title! It suggests you can make a success out of your preaching failures, doesn't it?"

"I don't know. I hope so. Let me read you what I've planned so far." He sketched out in detail the three themes he wanted to include. I listened ear-nestly.

"Well, Herbie," I said, trying to be gentle, "I think you're trying to cover too much. You've really got three separate sermons there." I glanced over his papers, and managed to decipher his scribbles enough to point out possible places for omission or reorganizing.

He accepted my comments humbly. "You're right. Now, why didn't I see that? I guess because I just jump into the middle of an idea and splash around in all directions."

I smiled. "It's the artist in you, honey," I said, "and I love it. But you do have to use a certain amount of logic too." I gave his shoulders a hug, and went on. "Also you tend to use too many abstractions. Like this sentence: 'In failure we have our greatest teacher.' Your hypothetical audience needs some concrete illustration of that."

After a few moments, Herb's puzzled frown dissolved into joyful discovery. "How about a little boy who tries to build a tower? When he places the final block on top, the whole thing falls down. Again and again it happens, and he feels he's a failure. But he finally learns how to make the tower stand."

We happily wrestled with the material all afternoon, and shaped it at last into something reasonably acceptable for his preaching class. As the electric clock on the bookcase chimed six, we shoved our chairs back, stood up, and heaved a joint sigh of satisfaction.

I had found great delight in combining our individual talents, and as I started for the kitchen a tremendous thought struck me: Wouldn't it be great if we could find a career in which we could work together?

Fumbling and Stumbling
(1939-40)

I must have been crazy to start out on a journey with no understanding about the destination. Worse, I had plunged into the exploration of the church institution without adequate provisions for survival, the equivalent of boots and food and maps. And most faulty of all, I had dragged Margaret along as a reluctant fellow traveler.

Even as early as mid-December my feet were bloody from the trip. I had stumbled severely over the matter of preaching. I felt in my heart of hearts that preaching did nothing except reassure a congregation that the old tried and true pathway was the only way to go. I knew that couldn't be true. Hadn't Jesus told his disciples, "It was said by the men of old....but I say unto you...."? There had to be a new way.

The other stumbling block in my early exploration was a class in New Testament. I had hoped and earnestly expected that here at last I would get acquainted with Jesus, the one man in all human experience that I admired most. Instead, enrolled in Dr. McCown's class, I was fed the dry husks of Near East archeology. This was my deepest disappointment with the school. I knew I would flunk the course if I stayed with it.

On a rainy Sunday Margaret and I rode the interurban Key System train to our field work at Grace United Church. I felt the time had come to be decisive about two problems we had talked about in vague generalities. Day by day I had watched my overdue term papers fall farther behind. I made excuse to myself that there just weren't enough hours in the day but of course there were; I just used my time for everything else.

The most challenging demand on my time was the assignment at Grace United Church where I worked under "Throcky." Thin of face with a crop of unruly dark hair, he was a warm, passionate, social crusader who had come to the tough big city slum hoping to help soften the horrors of poverty. I admired him greatly.

As Boys' Worker I had a dozen live-wires aged eight to twelve and I met with them three times a week: Thursday after school, all Saturday morning and as a class in the Sunday School. That took the biggest chunk of my time and called forth all the creativity I possessed. I felt I was learning skills that would be very important in the future.

But there were also other experiences that swallowed up my time: my scholarship job in the PSR library, the Wednesday night peace discussion group that met in our living room, frequent visitors who came to dinner and stayed for conversation, endless letters back and forth with Mother, and always, bed-talk with Margaret that kept us awake far too late into the night.

As the train clanked its way onto the Bay Bridge, and the San Francisco skyline began to show its jagged form through the rain clouds, I finally came to my moment of truth. "Margie, I've got to drop McCown's class."

She touched my hand gently as if to say, don't worry, but her practical words pushed hard against my determined stand. "But you will have to take New Testament sooner or later, won't you?"

"If I stick it out at PSR." That "if" was the big obstacle. I still had no firm commitment to the whole journey. But I *had* discovered another route for New Testament. "Anyway, I can get credit," I told Margaret, "if I take the course from a professor at the Episcopal Seminary next year."

We escaped the terminal, walked under her beat-up umbrella a block over to Mission Street and caught a ten-cent jitney. There were a dozen of those elongated black sedans that served as the poor man's taxi in the downtown area. They carried up to eight passengers at a time, and regularly saved us fifteen minutes of struggling with the trolley car system.

We arrived at our appointment well before Sunday School was to begin and enjoyed the peacefulness of the sanctuary with no one else around. The high, arched wooden ceiling creaked as the rainy wind pressed against the roof, and we listened, amused, while a leak sent drippings into a bucket near the pulpit.

This was the perfect introduction to my second decision. "That drip reminds me," I whispered to Margaret, "of the contrast Kunkel made between preaching and counseling. He said a preacher is like a man with a garden hose, spraying the congregation who are holding up narrow-necked bottles. He hopes a drop or two might fall in. But a counselor is like a man with a funnel who is pouring water into one bottle at a time."

Margaret twined her arms around my neck and kissed me resoundingly. I glanced quickly about the echoing sanctuary to be sure nobody had crept in to watch us. And then I told her of my second big decision.

"If I'm going to become a spiritual counselor, a psychotherapist like Kunkel, I've got to get me a funnel," I said, grinning. "I'm going to need special training, a lot more than I can get in class. I think I should ask for private sessions. Kunkel does provide them for some students."

Now that we were an established married couple, Margaret never failed to amaze me with her total support of any new turn in the path I wanted to venture onto. "That's a wonderful idea," she said.

With those two crucial decisions off my mind I was able to devote myself wholeheartedly to my class of bouncing boys. It was one of my best days.

Shortly following the holidays, with a mixture of shyness and bravado, I prepared myself to approach Dr. Kunkel. These were tense days in Europe, and I shared America's growing dismay over the hellish cloud of violence hovering over our world. This was the time of the "sitzkrieg" along the western front, during which the Germans were massing huge forces for their springtime campaign. I was secretly glad for the recent word Kunkel had shared with his class, that he had decided not to return to Hitler's Germany where his work would be under Nazi attack.

I lingered in the lecture room after my classmates had gone on to their next assignments. As Dr. Kunkel gathered up his papers from the podium, he squinted at me through his thick-lensed spectacles. His left arm had been shot off during World War I. He flapped his empty left sleeve at me in a gesture that reminded me of how life-threatening moments lurked everywhere. I screwed up my courage.

"I want to become a counselor, like you," I told him. "Are you willing to teach me the deeper meanings?"

"Ach? You want individual attention? Yah. Well, the best plan—can you come to my apartment twice a week?"

"I'll be happy to!"

"I need to charge five dollars each time. Can you manage that?"

"Oh yes. I think so. I'll let you know tomorrow."

I took the problem to Margaret, and we reviewed our shoestring finances, noting that we had volunteered to send ten dollars a month to Mother, and that Margaret still owed bills for dental work and eye treatments. We had only a few dollars left in our savings.

"Maybe I'll have to forget the whole idea," I said.

Margaret was quick to block my pessimism. She reminded me of the special wedding-present-account our friends set up to help us buy a radio-phonograph. She insisted we could borrow from that fund, because, she declared in her inimitable logical style, the special training was so very important.

I got back to Dr. Kunkel to confirm our arrangement. "And should I come prepared to take notes as with your lectures?"

"Not lectures. You will be in analysis. Together we will dig into your individual unconscious."

"Oh—"

My innocence of psychological methods suddenly lay bare before me. I was going to be pulled into a whole new world. The principle was that I could not expect to counsel other people unless I had been counseled. My private life would become the subject of our inquiry. Something deep inside me gave a sigh of relief. At last, maybe, I could begin to understand my confusions, doubts, and fears.

Kunkel added the final factor. "Your dreams will be the method of our inquiry. Each morning you should write them in a notebook. Write down everything you can remember, and then we will talk about them. Can you do that?"

On a bright, sunshiny Wednesday afternoon when my last class was over, I climbed half a dozen blocks up the steep Berkeley streets to where Dr. Kunkel had his rented apartment. The journal I carried outlined the record of several puzzling dreams, and my analyst-mentor gave strong reinforcement that I was doing my part very well. However, in that first session I learned very little about their significance. We went on to other problems that haunted me.

I told him of an emptiness in my soul that even my falling in love with Margaret did not completely fill. My boyhood had been a misery of aloneness. I felt I was a freak, tall for my age, skinny and awkward, a stumbler among my classmates, who nicknamed me "Big Head" or sometimes "Big Ears." My best friend, Danny, I'm sure in loving jest, had compared himself and me with a little jingle he had made up. "Little head, little wit; big head not a bit." It hurt me deeply. I couldn't see the joke.

"Ach," said Kunkel, beaming his enthusiasm. "Here we have the outcast image. Most everyone suffers this at one time or another. It is part of the ego's consciousness of separation."

I did not tell Margaret of my feeling of emptiness because I didn't want to burden her. Nevertheless, as the weeks marched on I shared with her, often at the breakfast table, the first run-through of a dream, and then at supper time, after my twice-a-week interviews, we discussed the interpretation.

"About last night's dream," I told her toward the end of a Friday evening supper, "Kunkel helped me dredge up some very important memories. He and I labeled it the 'Story of the Missing Father.'" As Margaret sampled a spoonful of our dinner jello, I elaborated. "I've told you how remote he always seemed. When I was ten years old and we lived in National City, Father made a try at relating to me. He took me into our garage to explain an invention he had in progress. It was a strange contraption of wood strips glued together, somewhat in the shape of a tiny chair, that was held by straps in a frame. He set it spinning and told me what he hoped it would do when he had it perfected. It would be a perpetual motion machine."

"A what?" Margaret's incredulous tone matched my remembered feelings.

"Yeah. Perpetual motion. Even at ten years old I had my doubts too. Kunkel is helping me see that my father was in a different world from mine."

"I see what you mean about the 'missing father.'"

After my next session I had an even heavier event to report. This one included Mother. I told Margaret how Father decided that my friend Danny and I were old enough to be introduced to the manly art of handling firearms. He owned a Colt 45 and bought some ammunition so he could teach us to do target practice. Dan and I thought it would be a great adventure, but Mother got word of the plans and squashed them. She didn't want her little boy to get the idea that guns were acceptable at any time.

"And what did Kunkel say about that?" Margaret asked with a touch of doubt in her voice.

I knew my bride had negative feelings toward guns because of her pacifist training, so I was cautious. "Kunkel asked me if I thought this event helped to stunt the masculine side of my nature. I had to agree. In fact, he stirred up other memories, how Mother went to the extreme of saying to me that men are bad! That only women have the true spirit of nobility and goodness in them."

"Oh, Herb! What an awful thing to say to a boy who was going to become a man!" Once again Margaret stood solidly with her young, fumbling husband.

A couple of weeks passed, and a sequence of cloudless days were ended by rain that pelted my slicker as I climbed the hill to Kunkel's apartment. The theme of Mother's domination came up again. I was grateful for his jolly mood and unfailing acceptance of everything I dumped on him.

"Sir, I'd like your opinion on something I've had to fight ever since Margaret and I announced our engagement. It's the pressure from my mother to make her a third member of our marriage."

"Ach, yes. Let's hear about it."

"I would like to show you her latest letter, which came a couple of days ago. I have to explain that she used to make a big point that she and I had a 'special tie' that nothing in the world could destroy. But when I got married everything changed."

"Often the case," said Kunkel and flapped his empty sleeve as he was wont to do. "Yes. Go on."

"She has complained, 'How can you be a preacher of good-tidings and at the same time fail in loving-kindness to your mother?' Anyway, here's a piece from her letter, and she refers not only to me but also to Marge and my brother." I read it aloud to him:

I could have had a few years of peaceful happiness and rest, if you hadn't blistered my soul with such cold, strange, non-human attitudes. Donald's persistent dislike of me is grief enough without hav-

ing your indifference and dislike added to it. And Margie—I thought
at first, that at last I was to have a daughter, but I fear you have destroyed that possibility by your attitudes. And I liked her so much.

"Well," Kunkel responded with a cheerful twinkle. "There's no mistaking
where she's coming from."

"What am I to do? She makes me feel so guilty."

Heavy rain rattled against the big picture window in a burst that reminded
me of the tears Mother shed to force us into sympathy with her needs.

"Not only do you have a 'missing father' you also have an idolatrous
mother." With that Kunkel opened a new chapter.

"What do you mean?" I asked.

"You have said she divorced your father. Use your imagination for a moment. Think of a wife who feels betrayed by her man. Her egocentric hopes
break down. Her ego resigns and her life loses meaning. To regain or preserve
meaning, she pours all her energy into serving her child, sacrificing for him.
He becomes her idol, a substitute for her Real Self. To take away her idol is to
rob her of her new ego goal, her god."

"Oh! That makes sense. I told you of her world teacher dream about me.
That fits in too."

"What you are doing presently is refusing to be her idol, and that is essential, not only for your own growth but for hers as well. You are on the path to
independence and freedom. Hold to it firmly."

The rainstorm ended as quickly as it had begun. Kunkel's analysis excited
me with new prospects of liberation. He struck a major blow at the ball and
chain that had tied me down for so long. I rejoiced.

For three months Kunkel worked with me, and toward the end of our
sessions, I climbed again the steep street to his apartment to report a very special dream.

"I was on a journey," I told him, "travelling on foot. I came to a mountain,
barring my way, but there was a cave, like a tunnel. I entered and went forward, but the walls and the ceiling pressed against me closer and closer until I
had to crawl on my belly and claw my way through the tightest of passages.
Suddenly I saw light ahead and came out into a most beautiful landscape."

"Ach!" said my analyst, smiling broadly. "Truly a classic image from the
unconscious! What do you think it could be saying to you?"

"Gee, I don't know. I do feel as though I am on a journey of discovery."

"This is the perfect image of a rebirth. You have successfully come
through a difficult birth passage. You should be able to look forward to a new
life with much more freedom."

My heart warmed at his enthusiasm, and as I looked back over the time we had been together, I realized that the promise I had dreamed of back in December had come alive. I was becoming a new person.

Doors began to open, matching my inner readiness to venture into untried experiences. Shortly after lunch on an sunny spring day, President McGiffert summoned me to his office. At first, my fears mounted that I would be advised not to enroll again; my academic performance had been very poor. The harsh truth was that I had accumulated incompletes in half a dozen courses, and a D-minus in one bluebook exam. My self-approval rating drifted slowly downward and now seemed poised to hit bottom.

"Sit down, Herb," he encouraged me. "Make yourself comfortable."

I blinked at the sunlight that poured in through his south-facing window.

"We've reviewed your progress," he continued. "I understand your decision to drop McCown's course, and some of the reasons for the rest of your current experience." He paused for pointed emphasis. "We'll be patient with you—for a little while longer."

My tensed up muscles and the tightness in my throat began to relax. I would truly be crushed if they decided to throw me out.

"How is your 'experiment' with the school coming along?" he pursued. "Are you ready to sample the full range of church life?"

"I don't know about 'full range.'" His question awakened again my doubts about theological education and the image of service through the church. "I've been feeling I'd like to specialize in pastoral counseling."

"You are not the only one. Kunkel has made a deep impression on many in your class." He smiled his strongest approval toward me, and pressed on. "There's one thing missing in your program that we need to explore. The school term will be over soon and summer will be upon us. You need to use that time to experience directly what it means to be the pastor of a church."

"You mean to be the one in charge of a congregation?"

"Exactly. Not like being one of the part-time assistants to Throckmorton, but full time."

As I caught the direction of McGiffert's purpose my anxiety began to rise. "But I'm headed for a career in counselling," I pleaded, still struggling to adjust to the excess of sunlight in his office.

"I understand. You've already made that clear," he said, as he finally adjusted the venetian blinds to soften the glare. "Being pastor is the best possible way for you to discover whether you can deliver spiritual counsel to real people in a real situation. The whole job in the parish includes counseling, preaching, visiting and religious education. You need to taste all of it."

I wanted to tell him preaching was not my bag, but he didn't wait for my protest. He plunged on.

"Now, there is a way you can do this. National headquarters of the Congregational Churches has a program called Student Summer Service. They can put you in touch with some of the small congregations that don't have a regular minister. These are usually rural churches. You could test yourself in such a setting for two or three months."

Here was a totally new prospect, something I had never, ever dreamed of. It haunted my study time for the rest of the afternoon. In the evening at home as we relaxed on our wicker settee after supper I spilled my uncertainties to Margaret.

"McGiffert says I should plan to spend the summer as student pastor of a small church."

"Pastor? You mean you would be the head man? Where would it be?" The eagerness in Margaret's voice told me she was fascinated.

"Don't know for sure. Possibly the Mid-West," I told her. "That was McGiffert's guess. Maybe South Dakota."

"Sounds exciting. Do you want to do it?" Margaret really surprised me with her big affirmative, like the cheerleader of a basketball rooting section.

"I don't know," I said. "It's scary. Not like the Boys' Club at Grace United."

I let the news hang for a minute, because the real issue for me was not the place or the job but Margaret. I couldn't imagine three months away from my bride. Could she accept my going off alone on such an assignment?

"How about you?" I spoke the words softly.

"What do you mean?"

"Would you want to go too?"

"Oh, I think it would be a super adventure!"

Her answer thrilled me and set me free. "But what about your job?"

She was optimistic. "I'll see if I can get a leave of absence."

This was not the Margaret of last August who dragged her feet as I launched my adventure with PSR.

My correspondence with the Student Summer Service office produced a positive response. I received an invitation from the Colorado Conference Superintendent, Nelson Dreier. He wanted me to serve in Cope, and my wife too, if possible. When I shared his letter with Margaret she wrinkled her nose in puzzlement.

"Cope? Where's that?"

"Dreier says it's east of Denver, about thirty miles from the Kansas border. On the edge of the Dust Bowl."

"Oh, my! A real rugged place! That's swell!"

I rejoiced that my mate showed such willingness to face the unknown. We had fumbled our way thus far. "But can you go with me? Have you heard whether you can get a leave of absence?"

"Not yet," she said. "But I should hear any day."

Here We Come, Ready or Not!
(1940)

Neither Herb nor I had ever been to Colorado, much less to the town called Cope. The prospect of spending a whole summer there with my dear husband enthralled me. It would be an exciting, romantic adventure.

But could I go? We'd counted on having my $120 a month salary for some time to come. It was our base of financial security.

Herb's salary for the work in Colorado would be forty dollars a month. A lump sum of fifty dollars for transportation. Housing to be provided by the Cope church. Those were the figures Herb received from the Rev. Dreier. Barely enough to maintain us through the summer! What about the fall? I waited on pins and needles to hear whether my social service job would still be available to me in August.

At last word came. "Well, it's happened," I said on my return from work as I joined Herb in our little kitchen. "Today I got the answer to my application for a leave of absence."

He put down the knife with which he had been chopping up parsley and green pepper for our salad, and faced me with full attention. "Well, come on! Was it granted?"

"No." I couldn't keep discouragement out of my voice. "They said I hadn't worked there long enough."

Herb grasped at a straw. "Maybe you could get an exception?"

"I asked about that," I told him, "but my supervisor said not. It's a civil service job, you know, and there are fixed rules."

Herb gave a sigh and went back to his salad making.

We ate supper in almost total silence. My mind was busy tossing around various alternatives. Herb could simply decline the Cope assignment and stay home to study and read. I wasn't sure he was keen about "student summer service" anyway. Yet I knew he felt the pressure of President McGiffert's insistence that it was an experience Herb needed to have.

What if he went to Colorado alone? No, not that! Our six months of marriage had brought us richly precious moments of shared struggle and joy every single day. How could I *not* be with my dear love in this new exploration?

The only other option would be for me to resign from my job. I was tantalized by the thought of taking such a daring step. Maybe I should!

As if reading my mind, Herb came out of his own reflections with, "You certainly can't quit your job!"

I kept silent, feeling a twinge of guilt. He didn't want me to quit! The security of my income meant more to him than I had realized.

As I started to gather up the dishes, I had the feeling he was about to give up on the whole venture.

But I wasn't ready to do that. There must be some other answer. During the next two days, I kept asking in quiet anguish, "God, what do you want us to do? Should we both stay home? Or should I quit my job? But I'm not sure what kind of job I could get in the fall. Which way do you want us to choose?" Over and over I asked.

As I rode the bus home late Thursday afternoon, a quotation that was familiar from my long exposure to Sunday School sprang into life and came to my aid: "Take not anxious thought for the morrow, but seek first the Kingdom of God, and all that you need will be given unto you." Aha!

I could hardly wait to tell Herb. We both reached Honeymoon Cottage at the same time that day, and as we went through the front door together, I announced cheerfully, "I've reached a decision."

We dumped my leather notebook and purse and his canvas three-ring binder on the setee. Herb sank into the arm chair and pulled me onto his lap. "Tell me, my sweet," he said tenderly.

I poured out my vision. "I think serving the church in Cope is an opportunity that God has...well, 'crossed our path' with. You need to go and I wouldn't think of not going with you, so I've decided to quit my job. I really do believe that 'the Lord will provide' whatever we need in the future."

Herb looked amazed at my strong conviction. He had often seen me "sit on the fence," vacillating, until he took the lead in coming to a conclusion. But this time my firm stance tipped the scales. "O.K. We'll do it!" he said at last, giving me an affectionate hug.

Then, with a mischievous sparkle in his eye, he added, "And the rebellious 'preacher's kid' I married is now ready to be a preacher's wife?"

I nestled close against him. "For the summer, anyway," I granted. My resistance to the church had definitely softened.

Now we had barely a month to prepare for our summer enterprise. Swiftly the required steps jumped out at us, one after another.

Dr. McGiffert, when he learned of our decision, had plenty of advice for Herb. I listened open-mouthed as my bewildered husband reported the unexpected mandates: a list of books to buy—or borrow—to take with us; the obtaining of a "license to preach"; a committee's approval for such a license; and finally, the necessity to belong to a church before a license could be granted!

This last was the most difficult for Herb. "Maggie, what shall I do?" he asked anxiously on Saturday night as we sat down at the dining room table to prepare for our Sunday School classes. "I feel as though I'm being pushed into big commitments before I'm ready. What if joining the church requires assent to some old-fashioned creed I can't agree with?"

"Well, why don't we talk to Throcky tomorrow, after the morning service?"

We did. Much to Herb's relief, Throcky explained that the policy of Grace Church was to welcome as members "those who believe Jesus is the Way of Life." He asked Herb, "Are you committed to following that Way?"

Herb felt perfectly comfortable saying "Yes."

As for me, I requested a transfer from the Oakland church in which—thanks to my mother's veto on my intent to "withdraw" five years before!—I still held membership, though "inactive." Together we officially joined Grace United Church the following Sunday.

As the month of May began, Herb came up with a new challenge. "Honey, we have to buy a car."

"Buy a car!" I gasped. I had assumed we could never make such a purchase until far in the future.

But Herb was convincing. "We need a way to get to Cope, and then to visit the scattered rural families while we're there." He sounded secretly pleased, and even I couldn't help feeling a glow of satisfaction at the necessity.

Throcky took us to a used car lot in San Francisco, and helped us pick out a dark green 1933 Plymouth sedan. As Herb drove it home across the Bay Bridge, he said, "Let's name it 'Budget,' because that $165 is sure going to stretch our budget."

I couldn't resist a pun. "And if it ever has problems, we may find we can't 'budge it.'" Even such a dismal possibility didn't erase the excited smiles on our faces.

We drove "our car" to San Francisco on May 5 for the evening service at Grace United Church. At Throcky's invitation, Herb had agreed to preach on that occasion.

Along with some sixty-five others, I sat in the pews and listened to Herb's winsome delivery of the sermon we had worked on together, "The Success of Failure." My heart swelled with loving pride.

As we plunged into our final week of preparation, Herb and I beamed at each other over shredded wheat and eggs at the breakfast table.

"Well, I made it through the whole year at PSR," he said gratefully. "I still have a few unfinished papers, but I'm making arrangements with my professors about those."

"And I'm almost finished at the Charities Commission," I responded. "I've really enjoyed my experience there, but now I'm more intrigued with my next commitment—to Cope *with you*."

Then we had to face a somber reality. "Mom will be arriving this afternoon," Herb reminded me, with a grimace.

"Ah, yes," I sighed. "She wrote that she wants to 'help us pack.'"

Mother Dimock came, she saw, and she seemed disappointed that she did not "conquer." I offered my mother-in-law a way to participate. "You could be a big help by preparing meals and washing dishes," I said. She had to settle for that assignment, but I could tell she felt "left out."

There were a few bright spots, but the undercurrent of Mom's unhappiness persisted. Her frequent arguments with Herb, her tears and accusations, shadowed the days leading up to our departure. I knew these confrontations were hard on him. We loaded Budget with luggage and food for the trip on the morning of Tuesday, May 14, and Herb hugged her formally, distantly. Our goodbyes were stiffly conventional.

As we drove away from Honeymoon Cottage, I snuggled close to Herb in sympathy and support. No bucket seats or seat belts to restrain me in those days! We were alone and at peace once more, and it was a beautiful spring day.

"This is the honeymoon trip we never had," I commented dreamily.

That trip was filled with beauty and adventure and rough challenges. Before we even got out of Berkeley, repair of a "bent tie rod" delayed us for an hour and a half. But I loved camping overnight in the High Sierras, surrounded by shrinking snow banks. The next afternoon a blow-out called for a new tire.

By supper time, we had reached Winnemucca, Nevada. Being a little tired of the picnic fare we had been eating so far, we treated ourselves to a cheap but hot dinner in a café.

Afterwards, Herb suggested innocently, "Let's drive a little farther before camping tonight. It's not dark yet."

For a dozen miles we enjoyed our ride through the twilight, unconcerned about the gray clouds gathering overhead. Suddenly I noticed a few wet streaks on the windshield. "It's starting to rain," I announced.

"In the desert? In May?" Herb, the erstwhile weather observer, could scarcely believe it.

Yet a few minutes later we found ourselves in the midst of a thunderstorm! Our poor little windshield wiper struggled to clear aside the heavy downpour pelting against it. A bolt of lightning struck somewhere on the road ahead.

"Oh, my God!" Herb gasped. "Too close!"

Thunder deafened us, and more rain fell in torrents. "I can hardly see the road!" he cried out between thunder claps.

I felt for Herb. As driver, he could not help being under great tension. I felt a certain anxiety on the surface, but deep within I knew a basic calmness and security. I put my left hand firmly on his thigh, saying silently in my mind, "I'm with you in this. I trust you to hold the car steady. We'll make it."

Herb gripped the steering wheel. Our headlights, probing dimly into the now pitch-black night, illuminated nothing but the center of the highway.

"That center line's the only landmark I've got," he said in a desperate tone, his eyes fixed intently on the white stripe. Without it, we might have drifted onto the left side of the road where some oncoming car could loom out of the darkness, or so far to the right that we'd slip into a ditch.

Rain continued to deluge us, lightning flashed, and thunder rumbled. Camping was obviously out of the question.

After thirty miles of pushing through the storm, I saw some misty lights ahead, off to the right. I tapped Herb's shoulder and shouted, "Look! Maybe that means a place to stay!"

He slowed down and turned into a driveway. The ramshackle "auto camp" had a vacancy! The manager led us through the windy rain to a well-worn wooden cabin, where we gratefully spread our sleeping bags on the sagging double bed. Exhausted, we quickly fell into the arms of Morpheus.

We awoke to find the storm completely gone, and sunshine streaming through our cabin window. Sitting on the edge of our creaky bed, we enjoyed a breakfast of oranges and bread and cheese. Soon Budget's motor purred contentedly as we journeyed through the "basin and range" country of eastern Nevada.

As we crossed over the crest of Nevada's final pass, we were in the midst of a singing a favorite melody when suddenly a terrifying noise broke into our song.   KNOCK-KNOCK-KNOCK-KNOCK-KNOCK!   It sounded as though the car was about to fall apart.

"What's happening?" I asked with alarm.

"Sounds like a burned-out bearing." Herb slowed his speed, but the noise continued, though with diminished decibels.

A bearing? I had no idea what that meant. "Is it serious?"

"You bet! If the knocking goes on too long, the rod could break loose and punch a hole in the engine wall."

"Oh." I didn't really understand, but I accepted Herb's authoritative wisdom. "Then we've got to get help soon?"

"Real soon, I hope."

We endured the nerve-wracking clatter and the uncertainty for fifteen miles. At last Herb saw signs of a settlement ahead. "Wendover, at the Utah state line. And there's a gas station!"

We made it to the station, engine still knocking and clanking. Hearing the racket, the lone mechanic came forward to greet us.

"You must have lost a bearing," he said with a knowing grin.

The man maneuvered Budget into his work area to begin his labors. Herb watched for awhile, then came over to join me where I had fled from the hot sun into the shade of a small building.

"We have a problem, Marge," he confided. "I don't see how we're going to pay for this. After the expense of the tire we got yesterday, and the one we bought last week in Berkeley, and the spark plugs, we have barely enough money left to make it to Cope. Look!" He opened his wallet to show me a paltry few greenbacks.

I was inexperienced. "Will this repair job cost a lot?" I inquired.

"Plenty!" Herb sounded really worried.

I didn't know what to suggest. My handbag held only a few coins. We were used to paying cash for everything, and didn't even own a checking account. I thought of a weak possibility. "Maybe he'll let us send the money later."

Herb heaved a sigh and went to hover around the ailing car as the mechanic did the repair.

The job done, our rescuer got out from under, did some figuring on paper, and handed Herb the bill.

Embarrassed, Herb described our limits. "I'm a seminary student on my way to serve a small church in Colorado for the summer. I will be getting some money after I arrive there, but I don't have enough now. I could pay you by mail."

The man raised questioning eyebrows, but before he could say anything, Herb took action. He removed his Longines wrist watch and held it out. "I'll leave this with you as security. When you get our payment, you can mail it back to me."

I was surprised that Herb offered his watch, the cherished gift from his elderly friend, Miss Hilgard. I couldn't help thinking, "What if the guy doesn't send it back after we pay?"

But the mechanic's response to Herb's drastic step relieved my concern. "Oh, no! Keep your watch. Just send me the money when you can." It did my heart good to see this man's trust in us, a trust that was justified when, in good time, we did of course send the payment we had promised.

Driving triumphantly into Denver, Colorado, on Saturday morning, we found our way to the Congregational Conference headquarters, where we met Nelson Dreier, our "boss" for the summer. After cordially supplying us with books and materials, advice and directions, and a rented typewriter, he sent us off toward Cope, a hundred and twenty miles to the east, with a cheerful, "You're on your own now!"

Highway 36 ran very straight through flat land. In the middle of the afternoon we passed through a town with the ominous name of "Last Chance." Still forty miles to get to Cope.

Immediately Herb noticed a change in the landscape. He cried out, "Hey! Look at that field!"

I saw a barren dirt surface lying two or three feet below the surrounding wheat fields. "What happened?" I asked.

"The topsoil's been blown away," Herb said. He slowed the car for a better look. A barbed wire fence and a fringe of weedy grasses marked the boundary. "We studied about this in Geography 2 at Cal, but I never imagined it would be this bad!"

He really seemed upset. As we drove farther, seeing a dozen more destroyed farms, I began to understand his passion for ecology. He told me how the great windstorms of the early thirties, coming on the heels of a series of dry years and decades of poor farming practices, had blown the topsoil from these fields as far away as New York. "The worst happened in 1934," he said.

I knew a little about this, from reading John Steinbeck's recent book, "The Grapes of Wrath." But my geographical sense was fuzzy. "Then are we in the Dust Bowl now?" I asked.

"Well, we've just come into the northwest corner of it," he answered. "Technically the Dust Bowl covers part of Colorado, western Kansas, Oklahoma, and northern Texas. In that whole region hundreds of farms were blown out like these." He added, almost ferociously, "No one should ever have tried to farm on these high plains! They're just not suited for it."

"Maybe you should have been a geography professor after all," I twitted him.

He shook his head with a rueful smile. But I was stirred to see the dormant ecologist in his soul coming alive. What a wonderful guy he was!

At last the gravel road widened, and I saw a sign, "Cope, population 150." Herb slowed Budget to fifteen miles an hour, and we cruised by a general store with post office, a gasoline pump, the school, several small houses. Herb made a U-turn and drove us to the store to ask directions to the McIrvin farm, the place Dreier had told us we would be expected.

How romantic, I thought, like a storybook! I was eager and ready to meet our new experience.

Coping in Cope
(1940)

Two competing experiences took possession of my soul in the summer of 1940. With Margaret, at last, I had my dream of a twenty-four-hours-a-day partnership. We were together in one common work, and that was my highest joy. But at the same time I was in a desperate quest to discover what my role in life was to be. Cope became the testing ground for the unanswered question, was I suited for the pastorate? Perhaps the path I was traveling would be a dead end.

I drove little old Budget about two miles over rutted one-lane roads, out to the McIrvin farm, painfully aware that reality was closing in on me. The land was flat, flat, flat and treeless, except for an occasional poplar that some hopeful farmer's wife nursed along in their yard. Aging barbed wire crowded close on either side of the road, and in the spreading fields, dry-farm wheat struggled against the odds to survive.

Our turn into the McIrvin driveway brought me face to face with what Rev. Dreier had said was one of the more successful farms in the area. It was not at all what I had imagined. The house was small, with corrugated metal roof, walls of vertical planking loosely sealed with narrow batts, unpainted, weathered gray by the constant beating of dust storms. It struck me as being out on the ragged edge of existence, as if it could vanish in a really big blow.

As we climbed out of our seats the dry wind pressed against our faces as a steady reminder that we now were out on the high plains of America. We walked around the house, toward a ramshackle barn, because we had caught sight of a human inhabitant. Mrs. McIrvin was busy at the hen house collecting eggs.

Our introduction seemed rather abrupt to me. I started with, "Hello. We're the Dimocks."

"Yes," she said, without interrupting her work, "glad you've come. You can go on into the house. We'll have supper at six. You will stay with us tonight."

That was it. Terse, efficient, right to the point. She made it clear that she didn't have time for the niceties of social intercourse. Yet in spite of her rough bluntness both Margaret and I sensed a warm friendliness. Her wrinkled face suggested a beautifully plowed field. She was strong in body and spirit, had to be to survive in such a marginal environment. The serviceable apron she wore covered most of her blue gingham dress

We stood, uneasy and hesitant, wondering if this was the extent of our welcome. She smiled at us graciously, with a sparkle in her blue eyes that said, "You'll get accustomed to us in time." Her spoken words were direct. "Make yourselves at home."

We headed back to our car and exchanged a silent glance, "What do you know about that!" We carried our suitcases into the living room and explored the compact layout of the house. A swinging door led to the kitchen. In the center was a round dining table. There were three small bedrooms. We had seen the privy out in the yard. That was all. It was extremely primitive.

As soon as I had caught my breath, the haunting problem in my mind came rushing for my attention: how to get a sermon ready for Sunday morning. I opened up my briefcase and staked out the corner of a small table to begin work, but I didn't get very far.

Mrs. McIrvin came in through the kitchen with her chicken loot and informed me in her musical nasal drawl, "Y'all will have to get used to our biggest nuisance." She wiped clean a space for me to work on. "We had a bad dirt storm early in the week. Still ain't settled out. Couldn't even see the windmill out in the yard." She pulled a cord on the single bare light bulb over the center of the table and was gone into the kitchen to prepare supper.

I turned to Margaret in my desperation. "You've got to help me, honey. I'll never make it to the Sunday worship. If you'll work out the hymns and prayers, I'll get started on the sermon."

She patted my hand gently. "Take a deep breath and relax," she said. "Whatever you do will be fine. Do you have a sermon theme?"

I stopped my rush, took several deep breaths, confessed that I had been scared stiff and gave my beloved a kiss of gratitude. "Yes, I do have a sermon title: 'God's Center White Line.' About our experience with the thunderstorm. How does that sound?"

We worked for an hour, until Mrs. McIrvin called us to supper and introduced us to the rest of the family who had come in out of the field: Mr. McIrvin and two grown sons, Carl and Ted. The father of the family was even more abrupt in speech than his wife. There was one feature of his face that I couldn't help staring at. His lower eyelids hung limply down, exposing the red tissue, as though all of the strength had been sapped out of them by the endless dust that had to be wiped out or washed out.

During the meal Margaret and I worked hard to keep conversation going, for it became clear that none of the family were in the habit of carrying on small talk. We learned that the primary product of their land was grass, to feed cows, to produce milk, which daily they sold to the cream station in the town.

Then I ventured to explore a mysterious sound that had bothered me. "Mr. McIrvin, what is that constant pounding noise we hear?"

He looked puzzled. Didn't know what I was talking about. "I don't hear any noise."

"It's that steady chungk, chungk, chungk, about every three seconds."

"Oh!" The light dawned. "That's the electric shock we put into the barbed wire to keep the cattle penned in."

It was a sound so familiar that he no longer heard it, but I kept hearing it and found it annoying and irritating, like a driving voice that kept saying, go, go, go, as though it were talking to me. Mr. McIrvin explained that the power for the shock device came from a couple of twin-bladed wind-chargers out beyond the barn, driven by the endless wind.

After supper Margaret and I got back to preparation for Sunday morning, while the family took their Saturday night baths in the kitchen. I worked until almost midnight to pull together my thoughts, scribbling sentences, scratching out clumsy phrases and endlessly shuffling pages of notes.

"Maggie, how does this sound?" I asked repeatedly, until finally exhaustion sent us both to bed.

After breakfast Sunday morning the family escorted us to the Cope Community Church. It was a small white boxy building with a steep roof. Mr. McIrvin, as chairman of the Deacons, made the introduction, and suddenly I found myself in charge: the leader of a church, the pastor.

The pulpit was a simple lectern, more like a wooden music rack. It stood in the center of an elevated platform, placing me eighteen inches above the congregation. They sat stolidly before me in wooden folding chairs. Only three or four of them were dressed in what I would call their "Sunday-go-to-meetin' clothes." The rest wore work clothing. All had come with curiosity to get a look at the new preacher.

This was not preaching class, nor the protected evening service at Grace United. Many hard-bitten faces showed the intense stresses of survival. Here was the real world of suffering people, and I discovered in myself a deepening feeling of unease. Do I have anything to say to people such as these?

In my sermon I told the congregation of thirty-five about some of the troubles we had in driving to their community from California, and from that drew a lesson, a plea to follow the reliable Christian "center white line" of faith whenever trouble strikes. I had no idea whether I connected with their thinking at all.

At the end of our first service Margaret and I stood at the front door to shake hands and be introduced to families of the congregation. Buxom Mrs.

Husenetter, with two children in tow, gave us a most cheery motherly welcome. A dour Scotsman didn't crack a smile as he encouraged me to pray for rain.

"Haven't had a crop in seven years," he said. He wore a short grizzled beard, and his calloused hands reminded me of coarse sandpaper.

"Glad to have you with us, Pastor," was the greeting of a young sandy-haired couple.

One young man, about twenty, delivered an earnest invitation.

"Good morning, Pastor. I'm Merle Rudnik. I hope you can come to prayer meeting Wednesday night at our house." His manner was markedly different from all the others, intense, emotional, aggressive. He had dark eyes and short blond hair.

"Thank you. We'll be glad to come," I assured him, even though we had not heard from Rev. Dreier nor the McIrvins that the church program included a regular prayer meeting.

After the morning worship Mrs. McIrvin escorted us to a house about a hundred yards to the east of the church, handed us the keys, told us this would be the parsonage for the summer and left.

We gawked with amazement. "This is bigger than honeymoon cottage!" Margaret exclaimed. "How do we rate?" It was by far the best house in town, a residence provided especially for the teachers of the local school, vacant during summer vacation. It was a white clapboard structure with a very attractive covered front porch of red brick. We could hardly imagine a sharper contrast with the surrounding farm houses.

As we stepped inside, however, we had to revise our expectations. The utilities were primitive. There wasn't any electricity. We didn't have running water. There was no bathroom. We had to walk fifty feet to an outdoor privy. We had to learn to light kerosene lamps every evening and to get water from a hand pump in the kitchen sink, after we mastered the art of priming it.

On Wednesday afternoon, with church list in hand, Margaret and I went calling, asking directions to specific farms from anyone we could find. There were no street names or house numbers. We were told to "Go about a mile past the Andersons, turn left on the north road and stop before you get to the gully."

By four o'clock we lost our way hunting for the Brooks' farm, stopped for directions and found ourselves talking to Merle Rudnik, the young man who had urged us to attend prayer meeting. No matter that we arrived three hours early, he would not think of letting us go on.

"Nice place you've got here," I began with the standard cliche.

Merle's dark eyes shone with eagerness. He seemed pleased that the pastor had come to visit. We stood awkwardly in the barnyard until Margaret, with her hand firmly linked to mine, picked up the cue. "Could you show us around? This is all so new to us," she said waving her hand at the scene.

Merle's thoughts clearly were elsewhere as he led us out into a fallow weedy field. His face reflected something other than farm needs. He kicked at a clod and turned to face us, declaring wistfully, "I often stand here for hours, looking up at the sky, and watch for Jesus to come on the clouds and take us all to heaven."

Margaret and I squeezed each other's hand. I couldn't think of any response that would connect with Merle's inner world. He seemed not to be concerned about the farm and food on the table and escape from poverty, but only about Jesus and salvation and angels in heaven.

"Most of all," he announced with great eagerness, "I want to become a preacher, to save souls, to help people get ready for the final judgment."

I knew Margaret shared the uneasiness I felt. Slowly the thought began to dawn that maybe I represented the image of what he wanted to become, and I squirmed, because I knew he would certainly change his mind if he knew more about me.

As the three of us stood in the field, we were joined by one of his younger sisters, Edna, a ten-year-old. She wanted to get in on the visit with the pastor, to listen to the conversation. Then another came, and more. Merle quit trying to introduce us to all of them.

He explained, "There are ten of us children. Johnny is not yet a year old. I am the oldest, twenty-one. Come along and meet my parents." He led us all back toward the barnyard.

Their house was not a house by my definition. It appeared as nothing but a basement structure with walls of concrete sunken down almost six feet and only two feet showing above ground. There was a flat tar-papered roof and a few coarse cement steps down that gave access to the only doorway. Perhaps it held promise that someday, maybe, they would build a real house above the basement.

Merle introduced us to Father Rudnik who appeared to be a totally unlettered German peasant, fat, indolent, unkempt, with unintelligible speech—a "Tobacco Road" figure. Mrs. Rudnik, with baby Johnny on her hip seemed more like a "Ma Joad" type from Steinbeck's story. Clearly she had no time, with house and children to manage, to fix up her tousled hair that fell raggedly around her face.

"Y'all must stay for food," she declared. "It'll be ready in just a bit."

The poverty of their world ran deep, and I realized that Merle, as the key manager of the farm with his mind and heart elsewhere, would never be a successful farmer. He would probably take them all into deeper poverty. I felt the strength of his desire, so different from mine. His was no experimental dream.

I compared my shabby vision to his and found myself wanting. And yet I also felt that he had no sound relationship with the "real" world. His head was stuck in the clouds; my feet were glued to earthy practicality.

Their kitchen occupied one end of the dwelling, with living room and one bedroom cramped into the remainder. Seventeen of us were crowded around a long narrow rough-hewn supper table that almost completely filled the kitchen. The Green family—father, mother and daughter—had appeared from nowhere and joined the crowd.

"Pastor, will you say grace, please?" The request came from Mrs. Rudnik.

I stumbled through some conventional words, and when I finished, a truly quiet meal followed. The children were not allowed to make noise. Margaret and I found the food barely passable: over-cooked hamburger patties, watery mashed potatoes, a few carrots in a lot of cream sauce, and chocolate cake. I was allergic to chocolate!

After the meal another family arrived, the McCammons with two children, from another town. They finished out the regulars for the prayer meeting. During the milling around Merle pulled us together with the Greens.

"I didn't have time to tell you before supper. Mr. Green is a Four-Square preacher. He's going to help me get to Bible college in Los Angeles, and...."

Mr. Green interrupted, "Glad you're here, Pastor. The fields are white unto the harvest. Countless souls to be saved." He carried on with his special brand of religiousness until Merle decided that it was time at last to get the prayer meeting started.

The living room of the basement house was also the main bedroom with miscellaneous couches lining the walls. Margaret and I sat uncomfortably on one of them. Under the pressure of people—twenty strong—it became oppressively stuffy and hot.

Merle, clearly the leader of the group, strummed his "geetar" for some gospel hymns that everyone sang enthusiastically. The lyrics featured words like "washed in the blood," "we'll meet in the sky," "saved by Jesus."

As the singing seemed to drag on and on, I heard someone drop the remark, "Well, when's something going to happen?"

Immediately I realized everyone was looking to me, "the local minister," to open the prayer part of the meeting. Nothing could have been more foreign to my experience in that moment. I knew instinctively that the formal intellectual prayers of main line Protestant churches would be completely out of place here.

"No, no. You go ahead." I deferred to Brother Green. "You know how you like to do your meetings. Marge and I will follow along."

Mr. Green accepted the invitation without hesitation. "While I'm consulting the Bible," he said, "let there be a time for testimonials." Several of the adults responded.

Merle stepped into the middle of the room, hugging his guitar, and poured out the most enthusiastic testimonial of all. "I am thankful that I can stand up this evening and say that I am on the hallelujah side and have given my heart to Jesus. And I pray that I may be worthy to go with him when he comes..."

His story called forth a chorus of responses from the group. "Praise God!"

Finally Rev. Mr. Four-Square Green gave an impassioned talk, calling for "more fire." His concluding words came as a loud cry. "All right! Let's go to prayer!"

Instantly everyone dropped to his or her knees, except for Margaret and me, and the wailing and crying that came from their Pentecostal throats shook the room.

Margaret and I were unnerved. We gripped each other's hand secretly, scarcely daring to breathe. Two of the teen-aged girls threw themselves so completely into the ritual of groaning and screaming that their faces became red and spittle dripped from their mouths. We were strangers in a strange land.

From where we sat on the couch I watched, especially, the three or four small girls, aged five to ten, directly in front of us, who tried dutifully to conform to the group pattern. In their ragged little dresses they knelt on the hard floor, squeezed in between the adults. They listened to the wailing and crying and watched as the older people writhed and twisted, trying to call down the power from on high. Clearly the little girls didn't know what was going on. None of them made any effort to copy. From time to time they looked shyly in our direction with a touch of embarrassment. I smiled sheepishly back at them.

With the group as a whole I knew we had come to an impassable language and experience barrier. For more than half an hour we sweated along with their passionate out-pourings. Suddenly the storm was over; the wailing stopped. They returned to their seats.

Mrs. Rudnik came to the couch and apologized for their neglect of us. "When you get better acquainted with us you will be able to pray the way we do." We nodded silently and fled back to our own world.

We scarcely spoke a word to each other as I drove back three miles to the security of the parsonage. Still in shock, we turned to each other.

"What in the world have we got ourselves into?" I moaned. "There is no way I can lead that bunch."

"The way Merle invited us, it sounded like a regular church activity," said Margaret.

"But it obviously isn't. No one else from the church came, just the two other Pentecostal families."

The following Sunday I preached on "The God of Love," a very restrained and philosophical sermon. We didn't attend the prayer meeting on Wednesday. On the third Sunday I included a junior sermon in the form of a fairy tale that had no reference to Jesus or traditional Christian language. It proved to be the last straw.

After the service Merle accosted me on the porch of the church. There was fire in his eyes. "You don't believe Jesus is coming again! You don't believe in the truth of the Bible! Not even the plan of salvation!" He clenched and unclenched his fingers in the genuine anger of one who has been betrayed.

I was stunned. I began a careful, qualified answer, but he broke in. "You don't have a call! You don't have the fire! You are damned! You are going to hell!"

He turned me into a speechless ninny. I opened my mouth, but nothing came out.

"We're through with you," he cried. "We're not coming back!" He stomped down the front stairway of the church leading his procession of family and followers.

It was schism! We lost a good dozen souls out of an already tiny church. What hurt most was that I had been unable to find a bridge between Merle and me. I knew nothing about the kind of salvation he was trying to win.

Margaret and I didn't talk about any of this until we arrived back at the parsonage.

"My God, Marge, what have we done?"

"Maybe it isn't total disaster," she said. "If he doesn't show up for the young people's meeting tonight maybe we can begin to make our contribution."

"But he will take half the kids with him."

"We still will have the other half!" Margaret took hold of my right arm as though to hold it up when I felt it was failing

Her faithful optimism always amazed me and gave me hope. But in spite of her positive approach I wondered in my own heart if I had what it takes to be a minister.

Really, do I know God first hand? Isn't it all just "head stuff"? What about our God Search? Who am I to say that what we saw at the prayer meeting wasn't a form of the Holy Spirit? Maybe it was!

By the middle of the week my discouragement almost turned into a rout. Only the intervention of Mrs. Brooks saved the day. Margaret and I found our way to their farm to talk about music for the next Sabbath. She served as pianist in the morning for Sunday School and church and, in the evening, for the young people's meeting. She was a bulwark of the church. As we sat in her tidy, colorful parlor the pressure in me built up. I simply had to pour out to her my anguish about Merle's announcement of secession. She comforted us.

"Don't worry. They came to the church only to try and evangelize our Sunday School children. They would like to seize control of the church, its policies, and its property. Maybe you have done us a favor."

Margaret and I exchanged a quick glance. Oh, so there was a lot more than met the eye.

"Mr. Dimock, there is a political side to all of this. The Pentecostals would like to install Merle as minister. Other families have told us they stay away because of the Rudniks. Maybe now they will return."

As we sat there in the muted light of Mrs. Brooks' parlor, radio sounds droned in the background. She turned up the volume so we could listen to the news. The British troops at Dunkirk had completed their escape from the overwhelming pressure of the Nazi army. An armada of tiny fishing boats had ferried more than 300,000 back across the channel to safety. We rejoiced together, and I began to feel that maybe I had just gone through my own personal Dunkirk. Mrs. Brooks had rescued us.

However, my sense of desperation did not totally drain away. Adult attendance dwindled. We heard the excuse that harvest season was coming on, which meant that work came before worship, but I knew in my heart the terrible truth that my preaching did not feed their souls.

"What shall I do?" I cried out to Margaret in the privacy of the parsonage. "They don't want preaching. They don't want counselling. They don't want Bible study. I have nothing to give."

"Oh, yes you do." Her answer came rushing at me with her confidence that the battle had just begun. "The *children* are eager for something to do during the summer. Your experience with Grace Church Boys' Club is exactly what's needed. We can start with a Vacation Church School."

I had never been near a VCS, but Margaret had shared in many during her growing-up years, and her instincts guided our labors beautifully. The boys and girls of the town would have been called ragamuffins back in Berkeley and Oakland, but here they were the promising future generation. No matter how shabby their clothing or unwashed their faces, they were our most important point of contact for offering loving care. They were aged five to fourteen, about thirty-five of them. Most of the group were church kids, but a very important minority had never been in church before.

Their hunger for guidance and new adventure was bottomless. Any project we proposed was greeted with enthusiasm. With them we did drama, acting out Bible stories. We built an altar-focus for the church sanctuary, with a curtain draped against the wall and candles framing a picture of Jesus. We went out into the dry river bed of the Arickaree and dug up a cottonwood sapling to plant in front of the church. We had a Fourth of July parade through the center of town, all in costume. Margaret organized a junior choir and a Sunnyside Club for the girls.

The climax of our summer with the children came near the end of July when the heat was fierce. We located an unused concrete cattle watering trough on a nearby farm. It was twelve by eighteen and a generous three feet deep. The farmer said if we would repair the pump, we could fill it up and use it for swimming. Margaret and I took turns with Budget to portage the kids for a wonderful week of splashing in the coolness.

And then our tour of duty came to an end. Led by Rosie Queen, our one fourteen year old, a blond girl who lived in a house trailer with her father, we were treated to a surprise farewell party. The children served refreshments of cookies and ice water. Then they handed us three simple gifts wrapped in newspaper: a small flowered table cloth, a salt shaker, and a stubby wooden candlestick. We were deeply touched, for they had told us, the best they knew how, that they loved us.

On the fifth of August we packed our belongings into Budget, and as we headed west Margaret beamed her sweetest smile at me. "Do you know what today is?"

For a moment I pulled a blank.

"This is the anniversary of our discovering each other at Lake Merritt."

"Ah!" The most important moment of my life to date!

And now I was approaching my Rubicon. We aimed our trip toward Lake Tahoe where, through Margaret's parents, we had access to a friend's summer cabin. She and I had not talked in detail about our plans for the fall, other than to agree that she would hunt for another social work job.

On the day after our arrival I grabbed my wife by the hand and headed down to the lake shore where huge, smooth boulders rose up out of the water. Margaret linked her arm through mine, and said, "So how do you feel about PSR now?"

"First of all, it's you who are making the difference in my dreams. I couldn't have done the summer without you. We were a top notch team, and I want to go on with that!" I peered deeply into the eyes of my mate. "I'm ready to go back to PSR. I'm going to buckle down to my studies, catch up on all my incompletes, and get the training I need."

Margaret squeezed my hand. "So the 'experiment' is over? No more 'maybe'?"

"Right!"

Apprenticeship for Two
(1940-1943)

Full of good resolutions for an orderly and "normal" life in the coming months, Herb and I made the trip home from Lake Tahoe on Monday, August 12. But when Budget took us into Berkeley in the late afternoon, we ran smack into a major surprise.

At the home of friends, where we were to stay for a few days, we found an urgent message awaiting us. Dr. Harley Gill, superintendent of the Northern California Congregational Conference, requested that Herb contact him "as soon as possible."

"It's about a field work opening," Herb reported eagerly, after reaching Dr. Gill by telephone. "We're to see him tomorrow afternoon at North Church, where he'll be attending a committee meeting."

"Me too?" I asked, puzzled.

"Yes, he said he wants to talk to both of us."

So I accompanied Herb on Tuesday afternoon to North Congregational Church, the building on whose steps we had sat together so often before our marriage! Dr. Gill excused himself from his meeting to greet us in the foyer. He was a bulky man, accustomed to exercising leadership, and his comments were direct and businesslike.

"The placement I have in mind for you is the Arlington Avenue Fellowship House," he said, motioning us to sit down on a short pew against the wall. He pulled up a single chair for himself. "It's a Sunday School and community center in North Berkeley, founded in 1932 as a home mission project of our Conference. We planned for it to become a church, but the Depression slowed us down. We want a married couple to head up the work there, because it is definitely a job for two. It pays $60 a month, and housing is also provided, upstairs." He snapped his lips shut.

My mind reeled under all this information. Did I want this?

Herb's eyes, however, were bright with interest. "What are the duties of the job?" he asked.

Dr. Gill described them briefly. "You would be responsible for the Sunday School and a young people's group. You would also keep the place open as a community center for the weekly Boy Scouts meeting, for the County Library three days a week, and for the monthly meeting of the Arlington Women's Club."

Hoping that Herb wasn't going to commit us to anything before I had a chance to think it over, I was glad to hear Dr. Gill's final pitch: "Why don't you go out and look at the Fellowship House, and then call me this evening with your decision." He gave us the address and a key, and returned to his committee.

I never liked to make decisions fast. As we drove along Arlington Avenue into the hills of North Berkeley, I tried to deal with my vague feelings of reluctance and uneasiness. We'd have to live in the Fellowship House. Could I accept that? Well, yes, I guess I could give up the idea of another honeymoon nest or a shared cottage with another couple. Would this work take too much time from Herb's studies? But I would be available to fill in while he was at school. Could I be content if I did not seek another social work job? Maybe I'd even feel relieved if I didn't have to! And I would certainly like to work along side of Herb! Maybe this job would be O.K.

But as we came to the unincorporated area called Kensington Park, one more reason for hesitating entered my mind. I observed the luxurious residences with neatly tended gardens—an upper-middle-class neighborhood!

"These people are comfortable and well-off!" I exclaimed to Herb. "We sure wouldn't be serving the poor and downtrodden here!"

He threw a quizzical glance at me, and I realized at once how egocentric and exclusive I sounded. I repented. No reason to cut people off from our concern just because they were "rich"!

Close to a small group of stores, we located the Fellowship House at the corner of Arlington and Ardmore. It was a large, old building with a gambrel roof, once a private residence. Its attractive gray stone exterior and the leafy rose arbor in front of the entrance gave it a romantic touch. My objections began to give way to a feeling of anticipation.

Inside, we explored the five rooms on ground level. My love of the old-fashioned responded to the dark-stained woodwork and the broad stairway to the upper story. Upstairs, we roamed through three rooms suitable for Sunday School classes, and a larger one furnished with a double bed and a bureau.

Herb had graciously held his peace while I was making up my mind, and when I said, "Living here might be fun," he looked delighted that I was ready to cooperate.

"The thing that appeals to me most," he confided, "is that this is not an established church, encrusted with tradition. We'd have a chance to be innovative and lead the way as we saw fit."

I was glad to see him so joyful. I hugged him, and whispered, "Maybe God does have a purpose for us here."

Swift developments followed. On Wednesday we moved into our upstairs quarters, and ate the first of many meals in the kitchen below.

Thursday night we met with the Directing Committee, the body of local residents to which we would be responsible. Before the evening was over, Herb had been officially named "Director of the Arlington Avenue Fellowship House," and it was understood that I would be his assistant. Thus we became joint apprentices as leaders of a community institution.

Little did we know what we were getting into! At first we enjoyed working together to organize the annual financial campaign, the one "tradition" we could not avoid. Together we cranked out 850 flyers on a balky, messy mimeograph for the Boys Scouts to deliver to homes in the area. It was, as I wrote to my parents, "lots of fun."

Herb's fascination with "leading as we saw fit," meant he was not satisfied with simply following a published outline for church school worship, or relying on simplistic stories with moral platitudes. No! He wanted the best for these open-eyed children, age eight and above, who looked up at him from the rows of wooden folding chairs each Sunday. He hunted for stories that would stir their imagination and wonder, or he gave fresh little talks of his own creating. The children loved him.

It was the same with the Hi-K Club, a so-called "semi-religious" group for high school youth for which we were advisers. Herb reached beyond the required minimum of just meeting with them on Sunday evenings for aimless social talk or ping-pong games. He persuaded them to invite outside speakers, introduced them to group games, and led discussions on real-life issues in school or neighborhood. Soon we were also chaperoning Saturday excursions like roller-skating or swimming, or evening dances at the Fellowship House. I marveled at Herb's talent for leading adolescents, and gave a helping hand wherever I could.

But the preparations for all these innovative programs were time-consuming. What had started out as fun had become unending responsibility. We never took a day off.

The pressures finally overwhelmed us. Herb woke up on a morning in mid-October with a sharp pain in his right side. "I'm afraid it may be appendicitis," he said anxiously.

I was frightened. What should we do? We didn't have a regular doctor—hadn't thought about needing one. But appendicitis? The very thought sent chills up my spine.

I tried to encourage Herb—and myself—to stay calm. "Relax," I said. "Take a deep breath. Stay home from class today." He managed to get dressed, grim and unsmiling, and ate a little breakfast. But all morning the abdominal pain persisted.

Toward noon, Herb phoned the school, and at Dr. McGiffert's suggestion made an appointment with Dr. Hadden, a young M.D. who saw him that afternoon. The diagnosis was "not appendicitis, just overwork— stress." Dr. Hadden prescribed a "soft diet" for a few days, and encouraged Herb to "take time off, lie in bed and read novels." I was relieved that Herb's illness was not as serious as I feared. He did try to rest.

One afternoon as he lay against the pillows on our bed with a novel in his hand, Herb commented, "This feels good. I really have been overworking. I'll never do that again!"

Silently I made my own vow: to trust God more, and not feel I had to do everything and do it perfectly.

We both eased up. With Dr. McGiffert's approval, Herb dropped one of his courses. Like an answer to prayer, a public school teacher came forth to relieve me of my burdensome responsibility for the Primary Department. We went to movies and hiked in the hills. Life began to flow more smoothly.

I thought we had learned our lesson once and for all. Neither of us realized that we had just had our first encounter with what would be a life-long challenge.

In fact, by the spring of 1941, our intent to reform had weakened and we again were "doing too much." One afternoon I was all set to drive into downtown Berkeley for half a dozen swift errands. I buttoned up my coat in our bedroom, and said a quick goodbye to Herb, who was bent over his study table. He looked up from his labors and said absently, "By the way, pick up a ream of canary mimeograph paper at the stationery store, will you?"

No sooner had I added that to my list than he thought of another errand, and then another. The room was warm, and I got hotter and more frustrated by the minute. When he added, "And stop in at the Gazette with this news story," I surprised myself with an anger I didn't know I had.

"NO!" I shouted, jumping up and down and stamping both feet on the floor. "No! No!" And I burst into tears.

Herb was as surprised as I was. When I saw his open mouth and the dazed expression on his face, my tears melted into nervous laughter. I took off my coat and sat down on a chair.

"I never did that before," I said, wiping my eyes and nose. "Where did it all come from?"

Herb came over and stroked my hair. "I've sometimes complained that you were too much of a mouse," he said smiling, "but I see you also have a hidden tiger. Maybe that's good!"

I was intrigued with this insight into my own personality. "Maybe so. A hidden part of myself. But I don't like to use the tiger on you."

He knelt on the floor beside me and took my arm. "It was really my fault," he said. "I got so wrapped up in planning this committee meeting, I forgot about you, my sweet wife. I was using you, as if you were my arm or leg—

or my slave. I'm afraid I've been doing that too much these days." We revised our plans for town errands and sealed with a kiss our resolve to do better.

Meanwhile, Herb had been slighting his studies. Conforming to the prescribed academic work always took second place to the allure of live projects at the Fellowship House. By the end of the spring quarter, his record showed many "incompletes." The faculty pressed him hard to catch up before September.

During the summer, therefore, with Fellowship House activities in recess, Herb spread out his books and papers on the ping-pong table in the west room upstairs and grimly slaved away. Day after day he ground out sermons, prayers, and scholarly papers. From the kitchen below, where I washed socks or canned apricots, I periodically heard the scrape of his chair and a few bars of cheerful whistled melody, and knew that one of the papers had been finished. All caught up at last, he took the stack I had typed to smiling professors. Not until a year later did he learn that if he had not met the deadline, he would have been "washed out," dropped from the school.

With a clear conscience, Herb entered his third year at PSR. He knew by now that, unlike most of his class, he'd have to attend for a fourth year to get all the credits he lacked through dropped courses and lightened schedules. But both of us were reconciled to that necessity. We were glad to be learning and growing, and looked forward to productive months in that fall of 1941.

Then the unexpected happened. In the late morning of Sunday, December 7, 1941, when most of our pupils had left the Fellowship House, a mother came belatedly to pick up her small daughter. Departing, she called over her shoulder to us, "Better turn on your radio!"

From the console that stood in the Fellowship House vestibule, we soon learned of the surprise Japanese attack on the U.S. Naval base in Pearl Harbor, Hawaii. Herb and I looked at each other, stunned. We drew up folding chairs and sat down to listen to the details.

I could hardly believe what was happening. Our long-time passion for world peace was based on theoretical ideas and ideals. Now reality faced us. A second World War, more threatening than the first.

Our shared pain deepened the next day, when President Roosevelt asked Congress to declare war against Japan. That was followed with war against Germany and Italy.

War or no, we were committed to producing a Christmas pageant Herb had written. We set aside our confusions and threw ourselves into the final preparations. Herb built a portable wooden stage a foot high for one end of the large meeting room. Women helpers made monkscloth curtains, to be operated by a system of pulleys and ropes Herb had devised. He directed the children in their rehearsals. I designed and mimeographed programs.

On Christmas Sunday morning, just two weeks after Pearl Harbor, a crowd of expectant parents were ushered into the rows of folding chairs. The entry hall held an orchestra of half a dozen young people and their instruments. A choir of children in broad white paper collars filled the stairway landing. Costumed characters awaited their cues beyond the stage, in the dining room.

I sat among the parents, enthralled, as the drama unfolded. Any children who did not have other specific parts, Herb had cast as a long line of "pilgrims journeying to Bethlehem." I felt a thrill move through the audience as the pilgrims crossed the stage, walking slowly, as though bowed down by life's heavy loads. A phrase in the carol we viewers were all singing, "O rest beside the weary road, and hear the angels sing," united us in a reminder of the divine source of strength.

A special magic infused that whole hour. Accompanied by music from orchestra, choir, or congregation, the curtains opened and closed on one reverent scene after another. We saw Joseph and Mary rejected at the inn that had "no room," the stable where they tenderly laid the newborn baby Jesus "in a manger," the song of the angels proclaiming "peace on earth, goodwill to men," then the visits by awed shepherds and wise men. I sensed the whole group around me responding in a heightened mood of wonder. Many had tears in their eyes at the close, as did I. In that historical moment of a world at war, the age-old story about the birth of the Prince of Peace touched the deepest yearnings of us all with new hope and faith.

The exaltation that both Herb and I felt on that wonderful Christmas Sunday was all too soon blotted out, however, by the flood of activities that inundated us in the first few months of 1942. The Fellowship House overflowed with meetings of new groups which all at once discovered their community center: a Civilian Defense Council, Block Wardens, Red Cross classes in nutrition and First Aid. Normal routines were punctuated by the weird wail of the air-raid siren at the Fire House, one short block away, announcing "black outs," when all lights must be turned off. Many Kensington residents took jobs in "defense industries," and others were drafted for service in the armed forces.

Whether we wanted to or not, we became heavily entangled in the war atmosphere that buzzed all around us. But always I felt a tension between us and the people we served because my heart was not in those activities. Hadn't Jesus said, "Blessed are the peace makers"? I had been raised on ways to make peace. In Sunday School I had helped send "friendship dolls" to Japan. I had denied myself ice cream cones in order to send money to Toyohiko Kagawa, the great Japanese Christian who wept when his country invaded Manchuria. I had been encouraged to think of myself as a citizen of the world. How could I now turn around and look at some of my fellow human beings as enemies we must kill?

Herb's feelings about the war were much like mine. He could not approve of America's entering into violence like the rest of the world. He felt fortunate that his Selective Service classification was "4-F," exemption as a ministerial student. Otherwise, he might have been sent to a camp for Conscientious Objectors, as some of our friends were. He did not volunteer to be a chaplain in the armed services, though some of the PSR students did.

We both felt inwardly isolated from the Kensington residents around us. We were again "marching to a different drummer," as Thoreau put it. But unlike simply choosing an unconventional wedding service, we were now challenging an institution much bigger: war itself. Our isolation and that "marching" drew us closer together than ever, and gave us comfort. In his sermons and community discussions, Herb now often focused on building a more cooperative world in the "post-war period." No one could disagree with that goal. I was glad I could feel in harmony with the rest of our community once more.

Herb began his final year at PSR in the fall of 1942 in good spirits. He felt in control of his studies, and graduation was now only eight months away. An additional PSR student had been hired by the Directing Committee to assist with the Sunday School and the Hi-K Club, so that Herb could preach regularly at an 11 a.m. service. His salary had been raised to $75 a month.

With all these things going well, Herb and I felt confident enough to "send for" a baby.

"We could schedule the child's birth for next July," Herb said, as we lay in bed on a mellow September night. "By then I'll be employed full time somewhere, and we'll be settled in a new home."

That sounded good to me. I counted back nine months. "O.K. Let's put in our order in October."

We stopped using the diaphragm on October 18. In November I went to see Dr. Lipsett, of the Stowe-Lipsett Clinic we had joined, and he confirmed that I was pregnant. We were jubilant, never suspecting what rough waters lay ahead.

The first sign of trouble was that I found my energy giving out drastically after only moderate exertion. One morning, in preparation for the afternoon meeting of the Arlington Women's Club, I started wiping down the stairway and its railing with furniture polish. Sitting or kneeling laboriously on each stair, I felt so exhausted I thought I'd never get the job done.

Herb had arranged to have his large, infected tonsils taken out at the Clinic during the Christmas break. Despite my scant energy, I went with him, and after the "simple" office procedure, I drove him home. His throat was exceedingly sore. I sympathized and waited on him devotedly while he sat in an arm chair and chewed "aspergum." Determined that he should recover well, I made sure he swallowed his big, red multi-vitamin pills daily.

Suddenly, after a few days, he began to spit up blood. A hemorrhage! At the Clinic, Dr. Lipsett put stitches in his throat to stop the bleeding. Guilt overcame me. Those big red pills had probably irritated the throat and caused the hemorrhage!

Herb had barely got back on his feet in January 1943, when I noticed spots of blood on my panties. Dr. Lipsett ordered, "Complete bed rest, otherwise you may miscarry!" But several days of lying in bed did not stop the increasing flow of blood. On Saturday night, while Herb was chaperoning a Hi-K Club Dance downstairs, I began to feel mild cramps, which continued all night. And on Sunday afternoon I lost the tiny fetus, less than three months along in the pregnancy.

We were both disappointed. But as I lay in bed for another week, convalescing, I began to get perspective. "We thought we were so smart, in control of everything," I said to Herb one afternoon, with a rueful laugh. "You can't 'plan parenthood' as much as you think!"

Herb's performance at PSR during the spring was remarkable. In contrast to his early flounderings, he was getting his papers in on time, and they frequently merited A's. He passed his "comprehensive examinations" adequately. Then he entered the annual Martin Dwelle Kneeland preaching contest. Preaching—the field he often wrestled with in such anguish! As I typed his sermon on the assigned theme, "The Cross of Christ," I was filled with admiration for the winsome way he portrayed the crucifixion drama from the point of view of a first-century Jewish carpenter who was ordered by the Romans to build a cross. He felt good about the sermon too, and looked forward to delivering it before the student body plus the judges, shortly before graduation.

When Herb's mother arrived in Berkeley three weeks before Herb's graduation, we greeted her warmly, hoping for a harmonious visit this time. For a couple of days she was cheerful, even enduring the lumpy sofa-bed in the ping-pong room without protest. She enjoyed recounting some of her adventures in Des Moines where she had been visiting her brother Don. Then the sweetness and light disappeared, and her old annoying habits took over, like criticizing my cooking and directing Herb to have a "clean white handkerchief" in his breast pocket on Sundays, ad infinitum.

Deeper still, she brought up her old complaint: "I feel as though you are shutting me out of your lives. Uncle Don doesn't want me any more, and neither do you." And then the central question, "Bert, why are you so cold to your mother?" No answers we offered could satisfy her.

Several times she threatened, "I'm not going to stay for your graduation. I'm going back to Los Angeles right away." I knew Herb wanted to retort, "I wish you would," but he restrained himself, and so did I, lest she charge us with further "rejection."

One Friday afternoon the intensity of the discord among us came to a crisis point. We sat with her around a small table in our bedroom playing cards, as she had requested. But the game failed to make her happy, and she pressed Herb once again to change his "unnatural attitude." When she didn't get what she wanted, her face took on a look of sadness. Her mouth turned down at the corners and her brown eyes were big with self-pity. She bowed her head, placed her hands over her white hair, and uttered a statement of quiet despair: "I might as well kill myself."

Herb and I were alarmed. As soon as we were alone, he said, "I've got to talk to someone. Let's go see McGiffert."

We drove to the president's imposing house on the hillside. The dear man was in bed, covered with bee stings, but he listened to our story. He had met Mother Dimock, and was well aware of her drive to control others. His advice to Herb was clear and definite. "It isn't right to crumble under her domination. When she threatens to leave, you should agree. You have to take the risk of her harming herself."

His words rang true. With our spines stiffened, we drove home. We met her continuing abrasive comments calmly and without defensive argument. Baffled, she simmered down. Never again did her threats have a hold over us to such a degree.

The next week passed in relative peacefulness, and on Friday night, May 7, 1943, I was able to sit comfortably beside my mother-in-law at the graduation ceremonies in the University Christian Church across the street from PSR. Together we watched Herb's class of ten march down the aisle in their caps and gowns. We listened with special interest to the announced results of the preaching contest: Herb had won first prize, twenty-five dollars! Then the diplomas were awarded, and Herb received his Master of Divinity degree— two days before his twenty-ninth birthday.

We fully understood that Herb's farewell to PSR meant farewell to being the Director of the Fellowship House too. Now that graduation was behind him, he renewed the search he had begun for a full time pastorate.

An exchange of letters with the Rev. Mr. Dreier, former supervisor of our work in Cope and now Superintendent of the Southern California Congregational Conference, revealed several possible positions in the Los Angeles area.

Herb was elated. "Dreier is really eager for us to come," he said. "That means he feels our work at Cope was highly satisfactory after all!"

He took the train south and met with pulpit committees of three churches. On his return, he reported that the church in Perris, a small town near Riverside, seemed the most likely.

"They want me to come and preach to their congregation a week from Sunday. If that goes all right, we're in!"

Herb's deep desire, I knew, was to shake off the student image that clung to him at Arlington and move on to where he would be treated like an adult. I too was ready for a break with the past. "Going to Perris" became the expectation around which all our thoughts and plans clustered.

In the late afternoon, a few days before Herb was due to head south to give his "candidating sermon," he and I were sorting clothing and books in our bedroom in preparation for moving out. The telephone rang. Herb answered it with his melodious "Hello," listened a moment, and then said, "Yes, of course. Right away? Fine."

He drew his brows together in a puzzled expression. "That was Dr. Gill."

"What did he want?"

"He's coming over. Wants to talk to us. He didn't say what about."

When Dr. Gill arrived, we met him at the front door of the Fellowship House, and invited him to sit down with us on folding chairs in the big parlor.

"I'm sorry to come in on you with such short notice," he began, in his businesslike way. "I'll get right to the point. I learned from Dreier that you are thinking of Perris. But—" He cleared his throat and adjusted himself on the seat. "As you know, we have been hunting for a pastor to follow you here and organize a full-fledged church. We wanted to get a big-name minister with lots of experience. Herb, I have to level with you. There isn't anyone. Many of the men are in the chaplaincy. This is the most severe shortage we have ever faced."

As we listened, the light began to dawn. He had come to ask us to stay!

"The terrible truth is," he went on, "that if you leave and there is no one to carry on, we will lose all the momentum of the past three years. The Directing Committee wants you to stay on full time and do the big job of starting up the new Arlington Church." He had made his plea, and his mouth snapped shut.

Herb and I looked at each other. Dr. Gill could see that we were jolted by this sudden proposal. "I'm sure you want to talk this over, and sleep on it," he said graciously, as he lifted his considerable bulk up from the chair. "But I do beg you most earnestly to stay here in Kensington." And then he was gone.

Back upstairs, we weighed the elements that would affect our decision. We sympathized with Dr. Gill in his tough spot. But were we the ones to rescue him?

"He wants someone who will organize a church," Herb protested. "I've had no experience with that!" Yet I knew he couldn't help feeling a pull toward the new frontier that beckoned. "There's something about bringing a new institution to birth that does grip me," he granted.

I realized we had invested a lot of our hearts in the people of Kensington, and in the methods we had introduced. I wouldn't mind continuing. "But there's one thing," I stated emphatically. "We'd have to have separate housing!"

Herb nodded. He reviewed with me the instruction given in his Church Administration class at school: that in a first parish it was important to be very clear in advance about a contract.

We finally laid down three requirements. If we were to stay, we must have separate housing, a salary of at least $150 a month (besides house), and paid secretarial help.

"If they can accept these, I think we should stay," Herb said. "I do feel a loyalty to the people here, and if we stay another year or two, that should get them over the hump."

Herb called Dr. Gill the next morning. In a businesslike style that rivaled Dr. Gill's own, he said, "Margaret and I have talked it over, and we have decided we will stay under three conditions." He listed them.

To each one, Gill's response was, "I'm sure the Directing Committee will agree to that. Of course." And it was settled.

I was relieved. "God works in a mysterious way," I said. "I guess this is where he wants us."

Herb formed his mouth into a crooked smile. "The irony of this is that we are only a poor second choice."

"Who cares?" I chuckled.

Herb gave me a hug and went off to send a telegram of regret to the Perris committee.

Parsonage Under Pressure
(1943-46)

Moving into our first real house was very important to me, for it was a physical symbol of my growing adulthoood: breadwinner, man-of-the-house, reliable citizen. But, as with all of life, compromise shadowed every step of the way. Finding any rental at all during wartime turned into a most daunting task for the Directing Committee.

The chairman told me on our return from vacation that they had to make a deal with the landlord of the only available house in the community. He put it to us point-blank. "If you are willing to fix the place up you can move in. Otherwise the bedroom in the Fellowship House is all we have."

Margaret was visibly dismayed, for our contract was firm on the issue of a parsonage. "What's the matter with the house? What is it that needs fixing?"

"Why don't you look it over," he said with a wry smile. "Then you can decide."

The Spanish style house at 671 Oberlin was built on a hill slope with seven different levels. At first glimpse it was definitely grand. There were four bedrooms and a magnificent living room with a high arched ceiling and a balcony at one end. There was even a box-grand piano included with the furnishings. But the place was a mess, especially the kitchen. The previous tenants, we learned, had been a couple whose marriage had collapsed, and the alcoholic husband had stayed on for six months. We could see where the man, trying to cook a breakfast, had dropped a couple of eggs on the floor and then kicked them under the edge of the stove where they dried and hardened.

I was thrilled to find that Margaret was not at all unhappy at the prospect but was eager for the challenge. We moved in and spent wonderfully happy hours during the rest of the summer, working together to make the place livable: dusting and scrubbing, painting the kitchen, scraping and waxing the linoleum, cleaning blackout paint from the windows.

By Labor Day we were in good shape, and while Margaret tested out her new housewifery, I began the big task of recruiting charter members for the new church. The first step was to craft a covenant statement acceptable to the Directing Committee. Margaret joined me in working on the first draft. What the Committee finally agreed to, out of their very diverse religious backgrounds, was a simple non-creedal form.

> For the glory of God and Jesus Christ, for the service of our fellowmen, for mutual assistance in our Christian life, and for the blessing of this neighborhood and our children, the undersigned agrees to become a charter member of the Arlington Avenue Community Church.

I had a delightful time through the fall and past the holidays, inviting people, one family at a time, to join, and by February there were seventy-two who had put their names on the line. We were ready to be recognized by the Bay Association of Congregational Churches.

But for me, personally, there loomed an even bigger challenge. The church, represented by the Directing Committee, had wanted my ordination to the Christian ministry to take place at the same time. This meant that I had to prepare for this along with my recruitment work. There were two steps involved. I was required to write a paper describing my religious experience, my theological training, and my beliefs. Then I had to appear before a committee of the Northern California Conference and present it.

At each stage of my struggle to fulfill this task I conferred with Margaret, and she delivered major critiquing and inspired insights as we developed the paper. I felt in the depths of my heart that we were crafting what should be called "our" statement of purpose and belief, even though the language had to be mine.

When the committee finally met with me in the parlor of the Fellowship House, there were six established ministers and Dr. Gill. I read my paper for more than half an hour, and then they subjected me to a grueling cross-examination that made me understand this was not child's play. I found the time with those men, my future colleagues, harrowing, to say the least. At last they excused me, so that the committee could "be by itself." I paced the floor upstairs in what seemed an endless stretch of waiting, and then Dr. Gill sought me out to report that I had passed.

I got back to Margaret before supper with my manuscript in hand. To her expectant smile I was able to give my good news. "All OK. Dr. Gill said the committee was impressed with my—I should say our—brilliant paper!"

But that news was not the whole story, and Margaret sensed immediately that something was troubling me.

"What else?" she asked.

I slumped into the big sofa in our living room and told her about the questions the men threw at me. Like, "If you were the chaplain of a bomber crew that was adrift on the Pacific Ocean in a life raft, what would you say to help them face their spiritual crisis?"

A frown creased her brow. "How did you answer them?"

"I didn't. I mean, how would I know? Hell, I just gave them some PSR Biblical stuff that.... Jeez, they knew I didn't know."

My bride's compassion was never failing. She came closer on the sofa and kissed me and held my hand.

"And there is something else much more puzzling," I continued. "After the meeting, when Dr. Gill told me I was 'brilliant,' he added his own special word. 'Herb, the congregations you will be serving don't want to hear about your doubts and your searchings. They want solid guidance on what they should believe. You've got to develop some convictions.'"

Margaret's face flashed fire. "What? You have convictions, important convictions. The paper was full of what you believe, where you stand. Was he saying that they want doctrine or dogma?"

"I'm sure that's what he meant. I can put my finger on the place." I opened my paper to the third page. "Here it is. This is the very heart of the problem." I read to her.

"On occasion I am struck with a deep urge to laugh or to cry (I hardly know which) at some of our efforts to contain God in words or thought. Our only true knowledge of God comes through being confronted by him, through feeling upon us his imperative to act, through acting. And this means that the farther we depart from experience into abstract language the more ridiculous we become."

"Of course," cried Margaret. "That's what you've been saying all along! So what are you going to do?"

"I don't know. I guess I'm going to have to try, somehow, to speak with more authority."

The next step in my journey into the life of the church came on the Ides of March 1944 when the Bay Association met at North Church in Berkeley to perform the ceremonial dignifying of the new church and their young minister. I delivered my paper for the second time, and the assembly voted to accept the recommendations of the committee.

When the business was completed and the evening service came to its climax, the Moderator called me to the chancel platform and had me kneel so that a semi-circle of nine ministers could lay their hands on my head and pray for the Holy Spirit "to set me aside" for this godly vocation.

Two things I remember from what should have been the most awesome moment of my life. The first is that the weight of hands bearing down on the top of my head grew heavier and heavier until I feared they would break my neck. The second was the feeling that Margaret, who was seated somewhere in the congregation, should have been kneeling beside me; that this ordination should recognize her also, for in everything up to that moment we had shared one hundred percent. She had been my secretary, sermon critic, typist, church school fill-in, janitor, errand girl, and even substitute preacher, once when I was ill.

After the service was over and we were back home in our grand parlor, I told her of the anguished thought that had swept through my mind. "You should have been ordained too!"

I was totally unprepared for her response. "But I don't want to be ordained. All that institutional folderol doesn't impress me. I'm perfectly happy to be a minister's wife. That's all!"

Margaret's bold rejection of my dream left me staggered for several weeks, until another episode opened my eyes wider than ever before. I came home from the Fellowship House office with the painful news that our Church School Superintendent had been unable to find a replacement for our primary department teacher who had moved to Los Angeles. I found my beloved at the parsonage sink preparing spinach for our supper.

"Honey," I pled, "can you take over? Fill in?"

Without turning away from the greens she answered with a complete lack of enthusiasm, "I suppose so."

The atmosphere in the kitchen suddenly seemed very heavy, and by the time supper was over I knew we had a problem. Margaret began the encounter.

"I've been thinking," she said, as we sat in the overstuffed arm chairs facing each other. "I kind of made myself over when I married you, you know? Some of that was good. But I've gone too far, so that I just follow along with your needs, and echo anything you think." I listened hard, and she went on. "That's not right! A marriage should be a continually creative relationship between two independent individuals, each of whom has something to contribute."

"What are you proposing?" I asked, bewildered.

"Well, I see that I can't let you impose on my time anymore. There are other things I want to do, that I have repressed so as to be a chink-filler for you. Most of all, I want to write. So, *no* I don't really want to teach the primary kids. You'll just have to find another answer."

I got the big message. Margaret would no longer be at my beck and call. She began her new vision about writing by starting a journal. But that larger dream was destined for postponement. In June we delighted to learn that a baby had begun to grow in her womb, and that focused our best attention on avoiding another miscarriage. On top of that, in August we received the jolting news that our landlord had sold the parsonage; we would have to move.

We celebrated our fifth anniversary on October 15th by moving to a pleasant house on Coventry Road, which luck and divine Providence had provided. Our first child was born February 15, 1945 while we sojourned at that parsonage: Jonathan Douglas Dimock. My confident sense of being an adult and now a father was exceeded only by my awe over the miracle of human birth. I stood at the glass wall of the nursery in the Berkeley General Hospital and stared mutely as the nurse held up the little bundle for me to see. And then I went to where Margaret lay in her ward-bed and together we rejoiced.

Now there were three of us to share the next steps on the path. The big good news of that spring was the ending of the war in Europe. That was followed swiftly in August by the gratifying end of hostilities in the Pacific. However, it was accompanied by the horror of the atom bomb, a new dimension of violence that was destined to shadow our lives for years to come.

For me the ending of World War II was only the beginning of the most intense warfare of my own life. Next the Coventry house also was sold. We had lived there just a month over a year when the Christmas season bore down upon us, and with that the beginning of a genuine homelessness. Now there were no new rentals available, none at all. All we had was the vague promise of the Elshire family on Amherst Avenue that we could move in when they moved out— sometime in the uncertain future.

Everybody in the church enlisted in the search. As the deadline approached, in desperation I wired the Gilberts. They had been among our early helpers in the Fellowship House and were in Arizona winding up a wartime assignment. Their house high on the hillside of Kensington Park would be vacant till February, they said. I carried the return wire to Margaret.

"We'll have a home for a month, anyway," I told her grumpily.

With the utmost good cheer, as she fed Jonnie strained asparagus in his high chair, the answer came. "Good. A place to celebrate Christmas in."

Her easy acceptance of our fate both baffled and supported me. "But we'll have to move again by February 1."

"The Lord will provide. He always does. Something will show up."

Nothing showed up as the end of January approached. Dr. Gill had told the church council that, in an emergency, the Dimocks could move in with him and his wife in their large house on San Antonio Road.

"The emergency has happened," I told Margaret. "The Elshire house on Amherst that we hoped would be ready, isn't. We'll have to tell Mrs. Gill we're coming."

"That's real generous of them to take us in."

"Humph! It's not just that. Gill was the one who persuaded us to stay with the Arlington project. He feels responsible."

Other jolts struck. The church had made major progress toward planning a permanent home for a house of worship and a community center, but in 1946 building materials were severely rationed, and the church-center request for lumber met with denial. We occupied a position at the bottom of the priority list.

Then came the news that a Mr. Hanelt had purchased the Fellowship House building and that he wanted us to move out so he could convert it into more profitable professional offices.

"Well, Margaret," I groaned after we retreated upstairs following supper with the Gills, "now the church, as well as the minister's family, will be homeless. I don't see how things can get any worse."

She took my hands in hers as we stood in the center of the room next to Jonnie's crib. "Well, we'll just have to be patient. Sooner or later it will all straighten out."

"Yeah. Sure. But the battle goes on and on, and there's no relief in sight. Church attendance is way down. People are discouraged. They're drifting away. Going to other churches down in Berkeley."

Our emergency home with the Gills stretched out to four months. The Elshire house on Amherst was still unavailable, because the home to which the Elshires expected to move had not been vacated. The Gills told us they were looking forward to summer visits from several members of their larger family. So we said goodbye to them and I piled my little family into Budget and headed for Yosemite, while the church council continued to search for a parsonage.

After three weeks of camping we returned to Kensington, and, with Mr. Hanelt's agreement, took up temporary residence in the Fellowship House beginners' room where the uncomfortable fold-out sofa provided a bed. Our old bedroom had already been remodeled for other uses. Then the Burtons nearby on Arlington Avenue invited us to be house-sitters while they vacationed. And in the middle of July, while the Hayneses of North Church were away, we moved into their parsonage.

August 2, 1946 I still look upon as the toughest day of my life. I drove our little green Budget with more than usual caution, down Telegraph Avenue toward the Permanente Hospital in Oakland where we held a group health membership.

For a week I had complained to Margaret. "I can't figure out why I'm so tired all the time. Climbing stairs wipes me out. I really don't feel like eating supper tonight."

In answer she delivered an unfailing confidence and support. "You should lie down and rest. This constant moving has been hard on you. Tomorrow will be better."

Tomorrow and tomorrow! But I got worse. The weekend came lunging toward me with the obligation to prepare a sermon. That's when I climbed into Budget and headed for Oakland. I checked in to Permanente with fuzzy brain; sat in the examination room; waited for the doctor.

The door opened, and a white-jacketed man with clipboard stood before me. "Mr. Dimock? I'm Doctor Arthur. What seems to be the trouble?"

I mumbled my symptoms as though talking to a tape recorder. The doctor laid me out on the sterile examination table and began his probings and pressings: eyes, ears, nose, throat, chest. I followed his progress with dazed curiosity, until he pressed his fingers below my right rib cage. My whole body jerked in a wild spasm.

"Your liver is abnormally enlarged; protrudes into your abdominal cavity."

I had never been aware of even having a liver.

"We'll have to put you in a room for testing."

"Will I be able to go home today?"

"You will be staying with us for a while. Maybe a week."

In the late afternoon Margaret arrived, having found a baby-sitter for our eighteen-month-old bantling. She held my hand; examined my face with a surprise I didn't see at all and only heard of later when she told me how woebegone I appeared.

"What's the matter?"

"Hepatitis."

"What's that?"

I recited what the testing revealed. "It's a virus attack on the liver. 'Acute infectious hepatitis.' But you don't need to worry, it's not contagious by touch; not airborne. Maybe water."

"How did you get it?"

"Don't know. They told me a lot of the troops coming back from north Africa were infected. It's not as bad as it could be. My skin would turn yellow, if it were really bad."

I went home at the end of the week, glad for a return of appetite. But an over-active conscience called me back to work. Tuesday evening beckoned, with the staff of Sunday School teachers needing my guidance.

"Margaret, I've got to go."

"Do you really feel up to it?"

"My feelings don't matter. The fall term is upon us."

"Well, all right. But come home early."

Both of us were deaf to the doctor's instruction: "The liver will recover in time with bed rest." We did not hear the double meaning, that the "live-r" was me; that I needed the letting-go of bed rest even more than did the blood-cleaning organ behind my ribs.

My sacrificial devotion to the teachers pushed me back into the pit. Relapse. Exhaustion and pain sat on my body like a rock. I called Permanente. The doctor became more than firm with me.

"Bed rest! Extensive bed rest!"

At the end of August the Hayneses returned from vacation, and still the

Amherst place eluded. The church council arranged a rental apartment for us in the neighborhood of PSR, miles away from our parish.

I had plenty of time, lying in bed, to mull over our life's pilgrimage and to dump on my mate. "It's pretty clear by now that my experiment with a career in the church is on the rocks."

That was the gist of what I kept saying to Margaret whenever she came to bring me my doses of Galen-B syrup, or to check on me between pushing the mop, doing our laundry, fixing our meals. She heard me, as always, but mostly her answers came only as a nod or a smile.

"I should face the truth that I never really had a call to the ministry," I repeated.

"Mm-hmm..."

"All I've got is a headful of theology. I think I don't have any personal experience of God."

She flashed a quick glance at my topsy-turvy bed-scene and went on with her chores, checking at the window to watch our toddler's explorations in the yard. I plumped up the pillows at my back, tried to focus on the book that rested on my knees, but to no avail. Margaret brought Jonnie in from the backyard and broke up my heaviness with a practical assignment.

"Can you read to this tyke while I get dinner?"

We turned pages in the "Golden Dictionary" to pictures of some food. Jonnie bent down and put his mouth over the image of an apple, pretending to eat it. I grinned in spite of myself and stroked his tousled blond hair.

After dinner Margaret took away my tray and put Jonnie to bed. I settled into my constricted world of rumpled bedspread and as she cuddled up beside me on the bed, I went back to my self-doubts.

"Sweetheart, maybe I should get out of the ministry."

"So what would you do instead?"

"I could go back, pick up again with soil science or cartography; get a master's in geography..."

"Those are things you left behind for good reason."

"I still would like to do playwriting, but you know as well as I, we would starve."

"Why don't we send for the Strong Vocational Interest Test from Stanford? You might find new options."

"What's that?" I asked grumpily.

"It compares your interests with those of sucessful people in various fields. I ran across it in my social work studies."

I pondered that for a while. "I guess it can't hurt to try it."

She sent for the test. I took it in my convalescent bed and returned it for scoring. I found a measure of relief, a hope that maybe objective answers might come to lift me out of despair. I lay back, pitched off the last residue of responsibility, floated on a sea of emptiness.

Who am I, anyway? As I lay in my bed, slowly I felt a Presence. Some One stood there close by my side. Day after day that Unnameable Reality brought healing to my body and to my spirit. I knew a deeper rest than night-time slumber had ever bestowed.

I knew appropriate language to describe this. I had learned it at Pacific School of Religion. Grace. Forgiveness. Redemption. The Indwelling Christ. Now there was a difference. The Reality entered into my tissues; filled up the hungry interstices of my soul. I let go.

Slowly I began to trust again that the future would unfold as it should. Day after day the sun rose with a new golden radiance to drive away the fog of depression.

On one of those very wonderful days of September 1946 Margaret brought in a handful of mail. A large manila envelope contained the results of my vocational test. I ripped it open and riffled through the pages, searching for clues to the big question: "What am I good for?" On the back page came a summary, and I read startling news, that I scored very high for the ministry. The report shocked me back into the harness I had been trying so earnestly to shuck off.

That became the moment when I knew I had been "called." The Stanford test confirmed what my Master had given in the vivid language of His love poured into my heart. I could do no other than love Him in return and carry on His work. The guidance came clear. I was called, for the present, to labor in a conventional parish of the Christian religion, the Arlington Avenue Church.

"Margaret! Look at this. An A-plus. I am where I belong!"

She put her arms around me as I rested back against my pillow. A big smile spread across her face. "Amazing! So you should do OK in the ministry after all!"

"Yeah!"

"I'm glad."

Her words further confirmed my "conversion," my recommitment to the dream we shared from the beginning of our marriage. Our falling in love had produced the slogan that declared we wanted a partnership in our quest for God and our hope to serve humankind. "Two can do it."

At last, with Margaret holding my hand, I came through my "dark night of the soul." The door to the future swung open. Whatever else might come of joys or pitfalls, my love and I would work as junior partners earnestly seeking guidance from the Senior Partner. Our life work changed from what we could do for others to what we would do directed by the Other. I knew divine magic had touched us.

The Path of the Spirit
(1946-49)

When we finally moved into the small white Amherst Avenue house on October 1, 1946, Herb and I breathed a grateful sigh of relief. But being in our new home didn't guarantee a smooth path ahead—at least for Herb.

To me, the path seemed smooth enough at the beginning. I was happy that Herb had recovered from his bout with hepatitis, and I addressed myself to the pleasant adventures of furnishing our dwelling. I searched the classified ads for bargains, and found a round dining table, somewhat wiggly, with four chairs, and a small green-and-orange-striped sofa with armchair to match. Of more elegant quality, a richly carved walnut bed came to our bedroom, an heirloom from my grandmother. I always enjoyed "playing house."

Meanwhile, I was also enjoying our little Jonnie. Ever since his birth, I had been constantly awed by his beautiful innocence, his alertness, his budding personality. Mothering him brought me a sense of deep fulfillment.

But Herb had responsibilities beyond our home to worry about, for the church was still homeless. With only the lower floor of the Fellowship House available now, most classes of the Sunday School had not been able to meet for several weeks. After diligent search, Herb negotiated with the Standard Oil Company to rent the needed space in a picturesque brick building near the gas station and firehouse. At last minute, the whole arrangement fell through.

I knew Herb was disappointed. But I admired his creativity in devising an alternate plan. Home study became the substitute for classes. I looked forward to his reports of how the enthusiastic boys and girls became "Seekers of the Way," "Seekers of the Golden Key," and "Seekers of the Open Door," by reading suggested storybooks and memorizing hymns and Bible passages. Parents and teachers were glad to support the program.

So was I! Having left behind my earlier rebellion, and my feeling of "Sunday School doesn't do any good," I was now able to appreciate the material that had enriched my own childhood years. It was through them that my feet had been set on the path of the spirit in the first place.

As far as the adults were concerned, however, Herb was distressed that attendance at the eleven o'clock worship service failed to increase. Hovering between twelve and seventeen, it even represented a slump from the previous spring.

"What is the matter?" he asked one Sunday evening as we climbed into our carved antique bed while Jonnie slept soundly in his crib in the next room. "Why don't the grown-ups respond as much as the children?"

I tried to encourage him. "Some of them do. Your sermon on 'divine discontent' this morning was wonderful, and they really seemed to be drinking it in."

"But there were only twelve there," he reminded me sadly, "including you and me."

Snuggling down into the covers, we delayed turning out the bedside lamp. I felt very close to my dear partner, and grasped his arm gently as I groped for some way to lift his spirits. I couldn't think of any great wisdom to offer. All I could do was express my habitual optimism. "I guess we just have to be patient a little longer," I said. "God must know what he's doing."

Somehow my fumbling effort helped. Herb relaxed, and turned to smile at me. "He sure knew what he was doing when he brought us together," he said. "Your strong loving support always pulls me out of the pit when I'm feeling low."

His hands found my bosom and I leaned my head closer on his shoulder. The window curtains reflected the lamplight with an almost heavenly glow, filling the room with peaceful benediction. I felt our souls had been restored.

Our bodies, too, had been quickened and we moved into close embrace. Slipping out of our nightclothes, we climbed to a mountain-top of delight in physical union.

That very night must have been the time of our conceiving. We had been inviting another pregnancy for several months and before November was out we knew that by summer a precious new little person would be part of our family. I felt we were richly blessed.

Soon after the New Year of 1947, our patience appeared to be rewarded. The long-awaited "permit to build" was granted, and suddenly the Building Committee, the church and the community sprang into action. Even church attendance crept up by a few numbers.

Herb radiated new energy and excitement during the busy weeks that followed. But at breakfast one morning in April, he paused with a spoonful of oatmeal halfway to his mouth. "It's wonderful how things are moving," he said thoughtfully. "But I'm not satisfied with my own spiritual life. I saw a new vision of my call six months ago, but it gets blurred by all this emphasis on the building."

I longed to help him, but had no idea how.

A few days later, a leaflet came into my hands announcing that a week-long "Camp Farthest Out" would be held in June at Asilomar, on the

Monterey Peninsula. The keynote leader: Glenn Clark, an athletic coach and professor of English, who was founder of the CFO movement. I studied the brochure carefully, noted that there would be "prayer laboratories," and was especially impressed with the invitation, "Come, bring your small faith, and watch it grow into a large faith." I would love to have gone myself!

I handed it to Herb with a casual suggestion. "Maybe this is something you'd like to consider."

Herb read it and caught fire. "Yes! Just what I need!" He looked again at the registration form. "The camp starts on June 15, barely a month before our baby is due. Do you dare let me leave?"

I pondered for a minute. I felt God meant for him to go, and I was ready to take the risk. "I'll be O.K."

Herb did go to Camp Farthest Out. In my teens, I had been to church conferences at Asilomar. I could picture Herb there among the white sand dunes, dark cypress trees, and rustic tent-houses, with the booming of the ocean in the background. I knew he would find it an inspiring place.

Jonnie definitely missed his father. The day after Herb left, Jon pattered into our bedroom first thing in the morning, looked surprised, remembered, and said resignedly, shaking his head, "No our daddy here any more!"

I missed Herb too, in more ways than one. I wrote to him,

"Solitary parenthood" is difficult... Don't think you aren't appreciated! Jonnie is so full of energy and pep. It makes all the difference in the world to have another parent to shift him onto from time to time.

Herb's exuberant letters more than compensated for my lone parenting:

CFO supplies what was lacking in my seminary experience. No mental abstractions and theology, but people sharing the hunger of their hearts, and their own pilgrimages...
I have learned how to use oil paints, and am finding deep satisfaction in doing landscapes...
Glenn Clark's spirit of calmness and faith overflows to everyone. He is full of humor too.

Herb returned home from his wonderful week, jubilant. After he had embraced Jonnie and me at the front door, he could hardly wait to show us some of his oil paintings. They were obviously the work of a novice, but I was impressed. Jonnie was curious. "The paint isn't quite dry yet," Herb cautioned, as he laid his big hand on Jonnie's outstretched fingers. "You can just look."

Later that night he had more to spill out to me.

"At Asilomar I heard so much evidence that 'prayer changes things,'" he said. We were in the bathroom about to brush our teeth; important conversations had a way of popping up during our most mundane activities. "I came to a sense that Clark is profoundly a person of prayer," he went on. "That is what I want most of all to become."

My mind echoed silently, "Oh, yes! That's what I want to become too!"

Herb waved his forgotten toothbrush in the air as he continued with a light in his eyes, "I had a private conversation with Clark a couple of nights ago. At the end, he put his hands on my shoulders and said, 'You shall be one of the knights of my Round Table.'"

He shared more during the next days and weeks, and I caught the CFO spirit myself. I especially liked Clark's emphasis that we are to pray earnestly for our "soul's sincere desire," and then "relinquish" the matter into God's hands. I was eager to practice this genuine kind of prayer along with Herb.

My chief attention, however, was quickly pulled to the fast-approaching "due date" for our baby, July 13. I got wrapped up in practical preparations—sewing curtains for the children's room, planning meals far ahead—and my intent for spiritual living faded into the background.

July 13 was also the date for ground breaking at the building site. I attended the ceremony that afternoon. The folding chairs were not very comfortable for one "great with child," but I sat through the lengthy program with fond pride in Herb as he turned over his shovelful of dirt.

Our new child "broke ground" exactly one week later. We agreed to name him Laurence Glenn, partly after Glenn Clark.

That's when the path—only a dimly "spiritual" path now—began to be rough for me. Required treatment for an unexpected difficulty with my bladder functioning lengthened my stay in Permanente Hospital in Oakland. The discouraging days wore on, brightened only by the short periods when our sweet, dark-haired infant was brought to my arms. Ten days. Eleven. When the nurses told me, "Tomorrow we'll remove the catheter," a cloud of troubling worries spun around and around in my mind. What if the bladder still doesn't work right? What if it never does?

Then I heard the woman in the bed next to mine humming a tune. I knew that hymn!

> All creatures of our God and King,
> Lift up your hearts and with us sing
> Alleluia!

I leaned back on my pillows aghast: I had forgotten God! It hadn't even occurred to me to pray, or to sing. I had been immersed in my physical woes and ego-fears. How far I had slipped from the inspiration Herb had brought me from Camp Farthest Out!

When he visited that night, I told him about my roommate's song. "I've repented," I said, "and I'm leaving the whole thing in God's care now." Herb took my hands in his, and we rejoiced together in a moment of deep peace. The next day all went well, my bladder performed normally, and I went home with my babe. I was grateful that my parents were there to help out. I was back on the good path again!

After they left, I faced the new challenge of taking care of two children at once. I had not expected it to be so hard! My physical strength had not fully returned, yet I tried to be a perfect mother to both small sons. Often I felt torn between giving Baby Larry the undivided attention I wanted to, and making sure his older brother didn't feel excluded. Sitting in a rocking chair, I fed Larry his "pablum" while I read a book to Jonnie on a stool at my feet—until he decided to wander away and get into who-knows-what mischief!

Herb helped with the children as much as he could, but his other "baby," the church, gobbled up much time and effort. My participation with him in the ministry we had shared so extensively diminished almost to zero.

The one activity I still took part in was the "prayer group" that Herb had started as a result of his Camp Farthest Out experience. This earnest gathering of individuals who responded sensitively to our vision of a deeply personal practice of prayer met regularly at our house on Monday nights. One evening I unloaded my frustration over never getting caught up on my housework, and my bafflement in trying to manage our two little boys. I found myself crying. The group members were verbally encouraging: "Oh, the housework doesn't matter," and "You're doing a fine job with your children." But the real salvation for me came through the fact that I had opened up enough to let them see my tears. They accepted me, tears and all.

Early 1948 saw construction push rapidly to completion, and on March 14 I left my two young ones with a baby-sitter and attended the Sunday afternoon Dedication Service. People from both church and community, 220 strong, streamed into the big community hall, which served also as a church sanctuary. I sat among the crowd and shared in the contagious spirit of joyful celebration that the building had been accomplished at last.

Yet a sense of incompleteness tugged at the fringes of my consciousness. The spirit of community cooperation, which Herb lauded in his sermon that afternoon, was not enough. Not yet had we succeeded in getting any great numbers of Kensington people committed to the inner life of prayer and walking with God.

We designed the summer weeks to nourish that inner life for the two of us. Herb decided to take the train to Colorado, to attend a "Pastor's Summer School" at Sylvan Dale Ranch for four weeks. "I'm hoping it will strengthen what I got at CFO last year and carry it further," he said as he kissed me goodbye at the railroad station.

Our additional plan was for me to take my turn with a Camp Farthest Out, which this year would take place in Southern California on the campus of the University of Redlands. But after Herb had left, my first plans for child care fell through two days before my departure.

I prayed a lot. "God, if you want me to go, show me how to swing it." I was led to the classified ads, and miraculously found just the right person to entrust my children to. I boarded my train with gratitude.

I had a thoroughly uplifting week at CFO. Glenn Clark was as fine as Herb had led me to believe. I loved Claire Boyer's guidance in our drawing with pastels, and Mary Welch's encouragement in creative writing as a soul's exercise. All campers became joyfully united as we sang unendingly under Glenn Harding's inspired direction.

Herb and I shared our separate experiences through numerous letters. From Colorado, he wrote to me at CFO,

I find the same thing true about the boys that you have expressed. To get away from them for awhile greatly enriches our love for them. I find my love for you, my Margaret, is also being touched with something new and wonderful.

In return, I exulted to him:

Camp Farthest Out is about the nearest thing to the Kingdom of Heaven I've ever been in...
     The leaders all love one another, and love us, and help us to love each other...
     You take any practical situation as it is, and pray for God to enter it, and He does, and the situation becomes closer to the ideal...

A peak contact for Herb was a personal counseling session with Nels Ferre, one of the summer school leaders, which he outlined to me in his final letter:

I unloaded to him my gropings and my hunger to find a richer spiritual life. He told me, "There is a man right in Berkeley who can give the help you seek: Charles Whiston, a professor at the Episcopal seminary." I will look him up as soon as I get home.

When fall activities began to fill the church and community center, Herb faced them with new resolution. "My goal for the year ahead," he declared, as he left the house one morning to go to his study in the new building, "is to deepen the spiritual life of the church." He added immediately, with a wry grin, "Beginning with the minister."

He did go to see Dr. Whiston, who welcomed him with twinkling eyes, and became Herb's "spiritual director" and life-long friend. I too profited from that connection, for Herb passed on to me what he was learning from this humble, joyful man. The central emphasis was "disciplined obedience to God." Whiston helped Herb chart a daily discipline to follow, and suggested types of prayer to be memorized for daily use. I was not able to stick with the whole regime myself, but the bits and pieces I picked up proved a fruitful spiritual resource.

Yet we failed to make progress toward our goal for the church. Herb preached on the importance of a life of prayer, and attendance slid from the 50's and 60's to the 30's. The prayer group which meant so much to us remained small. Opportunities that he offered for additional small groups met with no response. And all the while, his work as administrator of the community center activities soaked up the time he wanted to give to encouraging his flock's contact with God.

"The survival of Arlington Church is at stake," he exploded to me in October. "What is the use of a building without the spirit?"

Whenever Herb expressed his frustration and discouragement, I insisted that he was doing right to continue patiently focusing on the spiritual path. "Prayer groups will eventually grow," I said, with innocent faith, "and in time their spirit will spread to the entire congregation."

Both of us were blind to the glaring fact that Herb had barely begun the spiritual practices that Whiston prescribed. He was nowhere near being ready to lead the 170 church members into being a truly spirit-filled church!

It took a jolt to wake us up. After morning worship on a Sunday in March of 1949, Herb found me in light conversation with one or two of the last of the departing congregation. He drew me aside, and said quietly, "A committee wants to talk with me in my study. Wait for me in the car."

When he finally joined me in Budget a half hour later, the distressed look on his face touched my heart. "What's the matter?" I asked. "What did they want to talk to you about?"

He didn't start the car right away. "Something I didn't expect". He sounded stunned. Instantly sympathetic, I waited.

"They were friendly and appreciative," he said at last. "But they said in no uncertain terms, 'Herb, we feel it's time for you to seek another parish.'"

He started the engine, and on the way home filled me in with more details. The committee of three, who were some of his best friends and supporters, had said they represented a dozen more who had met with Dr. Gill the night before. They were all concerned that the membership was not growing fast enough and the financial support was lagging. They felt it was for the good of the church, as well as for Herb, to make a change.

"Well, maybe it is time for a change," I said carefully. My father had changed parishes several times, and it did not seem a threatening step to me. I reminded Herb how we had agreed to stay full time after he graduated from PSR. "We thought it would only be for a year or two, remember? We've stayed six more years!"

"I know," he answered. "And in a way it would be a relief to go somewhere else. It's just so sudden."

By evening he was in a mood to rejoice over the blow that had fallen. "The committee surely was sent directly from God, to nudge me," he said as we climbed into bed. "Through them, God has given me a clear mandate that I'm ready for something new."

The next day Herb announced publicly that he had decided to move on, and immediately wrote letters to set the wheels in motion to find a new parish.

The feelings of the church and the community were totally friendly during our closing weeks in Kensington, and culminated in a gala farewell reception in June. We were deluged with warm expressions of appreciation and wonderful gifts. The biggest gift was a tan-colored 1942 Plymouth, to replace our dear old 1933 Budget which was limping badly. We would drive that lovely new car to our new field of service, the First Congregational Church of Antioch, thirty miles east of Berkeley.

Mid-life Maelstrom
(1949-57)

By the time we transferred our partnership to the Antioch parish I was thirty-five, and I felt sure our marriage could weather any turmoil that life might send our way. After all, hadn't we come through the stress of organizing a new church, survived ten months of homelessness and emerged victorious from shattering illnesses, to build a great new church building? And hadn't we brought two new persons into the world: Jon and Larry? Surely, we were no longer stuck in adolescence. Surely.

Best of all, when the committee from Antioch had come to hear me preach, and after the morning worship sought me out in my office, their enthusiasm injected a large dose of adrenalin into my being. They wanted me. They were eager to bring a young minister to lead the church—a family man with children.

At home I told Margaret of my growing amazement over being prized in such fashion and shared with her the special challenge I saw in that parish.

"One of the men on the interviewing committee, Jess Allen, told me that a little less than a year ago the church almost closed its doors. The motion to disband failed by only one vote."

At this revelation my mate became strangely cautious. "That sounds like trouble. Maybe the church is really sick. Shouldn't you ask around?"

"Not at all," I countered. "Just the opposite. Mr. Allen said that over the past twenty-five years the members had become increasingly discouraged because all they had was elderly ministers who either retired or died in the pulpit. But now they're real hopeful that we can turn things around."

The day we drove into Antioch in our new used Plymouth I took great delight in playing tour guide to our boys. Jonnie was perched on top of our suitcases in the back seat and Larry sat between Mom and me.

"What's that smell?" Jonnie asked, and, in the rearview mirror, I saw him wrinkle up his nose.

"It's from the chemicals they use in making paper," I said. "Those buildings over there are the paper mill." I pointed out other landmarks. "There's the glass factory.... and that's an asparagus cannery." I detoured off the main highway down to First Street along the waterfront. "Here's the river, boys! See the big boat?"

"Boat," echoed Larry, standing up to see better.

"That's a freighter going up to Stockton, a hundred miles from the ocean."

Margaret sighed in a definitely positive way. "I think it's so romantic to have a river right beside the town. I'm glad we're going to live here."

At Sixth and F Streets I stopped the car in front of the First Congregational Church, a white clapboard building with a square, chunky bell tower. Several palm trees waved their fronds to welcome us.

"This will be our church," I announced to the kids.

"Where will be our house?" Jonnie sounded anxious.

"About six blocks from here," I reassured him.

Our move into the Antioch parsonage began the new drama in our marriage, a serious tug-of-war between Sixth and F and Twelfth and G. Margaret settled into her full-time job as homemaker and nursery attendant, and I responded to the parish hunger for new life, new nourishment to end their years of deprivation. Whatever I suggested met with instant enthusiasm. Teacher training sessions? Yes! How about a men's club? Of course! A regular printed newsletter? Great!

To Margaret I confided, "It's rather dazzling, all this eagerness and cooperation. Sort of like a honeymoon."

I found myself pulled in deeper and deeper, not realizing that the more time I spent with the church, the less time I had to give to my home, not remembering that when it came to work I was an addict, in company with millions of other American males.

The needs of the parish, I found, were tied into the whole town and that connection hit me like a whirlwind, sucking me into a dozen activities I had never dreamed of.

Early in 1950 the Ministerial Association chose me to be their chairman. Offering an invocation for meetings of the Antioch city council loomed as one of our collective chores. I had to schedule ten ministers in rotation, and I was the one to fill in when one of them called at the last minute, praying to be excused. Also I had oversight of the fifteen minute Morning Devotional at the local radio station.

On the heels of that chairmanship, the region's Council of Churches called me into leadership, and I pulled together a program to celebrate the centennial of the city of Antioch, now grown to a town of ten thousand.

These assignments boosted my self-image and the prestige of the Congregational Church as a provider of professional skills to the community.

One Spring day I walked home from the office and found lunch preparations had been delayed. Margaret was sitting in our breakfast nook sipping buttermilk. The smile on her face invited me to sit opposite with my big question, for I knew she had been to the doctor's.

Her answer was, "Yes. The baby will be due in late January."

Our lunch that day turned into a quickie, because I had a one o'clock appointment to give marriage counseling to a distressed young couple.

I had begun to discover that the need for counseling of all sorts was massive in this town. Apparently word-of-mouth information got around that the pastor of the Congregational Church had a willing ear. Ever since my days with Fritz Kunkel at PSR, I had wanted to be a counselor. Now life tested me to see what I could produce. I couldn't have asked for more if I had hung out my shingle.

Over the months and years couples came for help, and I groped for how I could lead them into a happy marriage such as, I wanted them to know, Margaret and I enjoyed. Frequently a desperate wife would get on the phone and cry for help. One unforgettable call pulled me into a warring home, and suddenly I found myself directly between the couple who had armed themselves with butcher knife and flatiron. I yelled at them to back off, focusing especially on the husband. Then I got on the phone and called the police and had the man hauled into court where the judge and I set up a system to help the family work at conflict resolution. This was not exactly "spiritual counseling." In the long run I discovered nothing would really help this particular couple.

The pace of my parish work accelerated. Soon we instituted two services of worship on Sunday morning. These were the fabulous Fifties for churches, right across the nation. In the aftermath of World War II, and with the onset of the Korean War, a great deal of soul searching developed. We organized Bible study classes and prayer groups. Also, our lay people became involved in sponsoring several Displaced Person families from post-war Europe. We contributed generously to the Heifers for Japan program to help rebuild the herds destroyed by the war. I persisted in bringing famous names to deliver their messages to the local community: Glenn Clark, Starr Daily, Rebecca Beard, and Frank Laubach.

And then in addition to all the other programs, our Men's Club proposed that we do a major enlargement of the old building to meet our growing needs. Abruptly I found myself back in the intense cycle that had ruled my life in Arlington: architects, contractors, building fund appeals.

Our marriage suffered. My times at home became more and more sparse. I struggled to make time for dates with Jon and Larry, for I determined that they should not be totally neglected by their father. Once a week I took one or the other on some kind of excursion. With Larry I pursued his hobby of collecting bullet slugs at the local rifle range. I once did a major trip with Jon to San Francisco to take in a movie. But generally the score added up to serious neglect for the family.

The terrible irony of my life lurked just beyond my sight. How could I possibly help the several men who were addicted to alcohol when I couldn't escape my own addiction?

The Lenten season each year regularly produced the high tide of my efforts. That particular year I must have worked on a dozen fronts, feverishly. The week after Easter I headed for Berkeley for my monthly visit to my spiritual director, Dr. Whiston. The little notebook in my hand contained the record of my prayer discipline. As I arrived at the door of my mentor's home it dawned on me that my story would not look very good. I almost wanted to lose the notebook, but the door opened, and we sat together, with Whiston thumbing through the pages. Finally he looked up at me.

"Herb, what is the meaning of this? Day after day there are big blank spots. Didn't you pray at all during Lent?"

Awkwardly I explained about how busy I had been. He was not impressed at all.

"Lent is the time of all times when we should be faithful to the Christ. It was during these weeks that he went through his most intense suffering!"

My mouth went dry, and I tried to figure a way to justify my behavior. But nothing worked. He pressed even harder.

"Here the record shows that you hardly prayed at all for your parishioners. Can you tell me why all these other things you say you have been doing are more important than praying for your people?"

Firmly and with stern sadness in his voice, he poured out the final judgment. "Herb, this is spiritual sloth! There is no excuse for this."

I returned to Antioch chastened, and I vowed never again to give the demands of church administration any precedence over the spiritual work that is the most important function of a pastor. I vowed to start with my family, to be faithful to my spiritual discipline for their sake.

When Martha was born, Margaret and I were ecstatic over our daughter, a pixie with dancing brown eyes. But Mama's role in the nursery made a quantum leap. She was swamped by the waves of child care that washed over her, while month after month I yielded to what I believed the parish and the community needed to survive and grow. We drifted further into parallel lives. Two separate careers. Two worlds that touched briefly at mealtimes.

Often when I returned home from a late evening committee meeting Margaret would already be in bed, sound asleep. I resisted my need to waken her. Our marriage bed seemed more like a remote dream than a present opportunity. By the time Martha turned three we relinquished our bedroom to her and took up residence in the creaky fold-down wall bed in the dining room.

My loneliness deepened. My work at the church began to show the effects in ways that escaped my attention. It came to me as a major shock that more than one of my lay people saw my problem, and acted on what they saw. Two of them were women.

"Janet" came to my office, which did not generally serve well as a counseling room, because my secretary could hear everything through a very thin door. I had previously helped Janet through some tough spiritual problems.

"Herb, do you have time to talk?"

"Sure. Do you want..."

"Can we go to the sanctuary?"

We sat in the front pew, facing the recently rebuilt chancel, with warm light streaming through the stained glass.

"I'm concerned about you."

For the first time in my counseling career I became the counselee. "Have I offended someone?" That was my leading thought.

"Not that. I've been observing you week after week. You seem to be wandering to and fro among the people of the congregation, wistfully hunting for something. Something that you never seem to find. What is the matter?"

I felt a burning sensation behind my eyelids, and my tongue delivered some kind of meaningless cover-up. I myself didn't know how deep was my trouble. No way could I talk about the desert that spread between myself and my spouse.

Our conversation in the sanctuary that day jolted me to begin paying attention. To ask the impossible question, "Is our marriage headed for the rocks?" I did not tell Margaret of my encounter with Janet right away.

The second woman, about my own age, "Mary," also came to the office, and her style could not have been more polar. My secretary had left for the day. I sat alone in my swivel chair. Mary, with deep and womanly warmth, stood close, looked down at me and put her arms around my head. She drew me close and stroked my hair.

The moment utterly overwhelmed me. I could not tell whether this was a lover's caress or a mother's. My instinct moved me to shift us over to the sanctuary again, where the chance of being interrupted would recede. We sat in the same front pew. Mary did not talk analytically the way Janet had. Affectionate concern for her pastor came pouring out and baffled me utterly.

I went home to Margaret. Immediately, with no detail omitted, I unloaded both experiences, because I sensed how easy it would be to cross over into forbidden terrain.

My beloved took it all in stride, confident of my faithfulness. But I will never forget her last comment, which burst tearfully from her lips and told of her own deep distress.

"You didn't have to kiss her!"

My loneliness didn't go away. It slipped down into a kind of limbo. We didn't talk about Mary and Janet, or the hidden sexual agenda we had stumbled into. However, two things did develop in quick succession. I told Mary that I had told Margaret exactly what had happened between us. Mary's reaction came out predictably. Shock, awakening, regret. One thing my instincts had told me accurately, secrets would be dangerous. We pushed everything out into the open. In time that helped Margaret and Mary to come to their own understanding and reconciliation.

The second development came a couple of weeks later as I took my lunch break with Margaret. Both boys were at school and Martha was at a playmate's house. I slipped into our well-worn breakfast nook off the kitchen, as Margaret laid out our soup and sandwiches. We held hands across the table for a grace-moment, and I went to work on the food. But Margaret didn't. She sat quietly watching me eat.

"Is something the matter, Maggie?" I asked.

"I had a visitor this morning."

Something about her eyes told me to pay more than casual attention. "Visitor?"

"Sonja. You know, the woman who volunteered to help in the kindergarten."

"Problems with the children?"

"Not children. We sat together in the living room, and right away she threw me a big surprise. She said, 'I want to apologize to you.'"

"For what?" I said, as I laid my sandwich down to catch all the nuances of the story.

"That's what I asked her, and her answer was, 'I've always admired your husband, but I feel as though I'm intruding into your territory. I haven't done anything he would know about. It's just that I have such deep feelings of attraction toward him. Things I shouldn't be feeling. After all, he's your husband.' She really showed she was terribly upset!"

"What did you say to her?"

"I sure felt awkward," Margaret muttered. "All I could think to say was that I hadn't noticed anything. But she went on, 'Just the same, I need to apologize. Will you forgive me?' Well, of course I said I would, if there was anything to forgive."

"Wow," I groaned. "Sonja showed a lot of courage to come to you with that kind of stuff!"

"But that wasn't all. The rest of what happened..." Margaret shook her head, groping for words. "I've never heard anything like... I mean, Sonja poured out the rest of her story this way. 'I think I should tell you that when I sit in the pew, and he is preaching, very often I see a glow of white light around him.'"

"What?" I exclaimed.

Margaret spread out her hands in a silent gesture of wonder. We sensed we had crossed over into a new area of experience and didn't know how to relate to it. Somehow we finished up on lunch, and I headed back toward the office, but I never arrived. My feet took me on a long walk of inner exploration.

I checked over in memory a dozen encounters with women parishioners, in counseling sessions, in Bible classes, in home visits, and began to see, as I had never noticed before, subtle signs of attraction that were outside the formal bounds of organized religion. The professional minister is still a man, and when he preaches about love, and shows a demeanor of tender compassionate caring, a woman can very easily respond with a "sexual spirituality." What a maelstrom! Life had plunged me into more than I could manage.

All of this had a profound impact on our marriage, and, at long last, a moment came when life led us to confrontation. School had recessed for the summer. Jon had diminished his aggressive teasing of Larry. Martha was looking forward to kindergarten in the fall. The day was Monday, my day off. A good outing was long overdue for all of us. Margaret packed a picnic hamper, and we drove across the Antioch bridge to Sherman Island, one of the last of the low-lying islands of the Delta. We had a thinly overcast sky to shelter us. I turned off the highway and followed a dirt road, through the agricultural setting, to the end where we parked. We could look back across the river toward our town a half-mile away. The children got out their pails and shovels to play on the sandy beach. Quickly they stripped off their shoes and socks to go wading in the water. Margaret and I sat in the front seat of the car.

I slipped an arm around her shoulder and drew her close. My first words were heaven-inspired and totally ordinary. "How are things going with you?" Somehow I had been moved to put my own concerns on the back burner.

Tears trickled out of her eyes, tears of relief, that I cared, and that at last we could talk. "The daily schedule you suggested for me has helped some, but I still seem to have too much to do. I never really have a chance to relax or rest."

I sealed my lips and waited.

"I've been trying to work at what Janet said to me about not letting the children run my life, but I'm not doing very well."

The scene at the edge of the sand in that moment exploded as Jonnie carelessly kicked water onto Martha. I felt Margaret instantly mobilizing her police function to climb out of the car and restrain the offender. I laid a hand on her leg.

"No. Leave them alone. They'll work it out."

She relaxed with a groan. "My habits are so strong."

"You've had to work at a solo job," I ventured, for my sensitivity to her pain had come to the surface.

"But I always know you're there." She looked up at me with a wistful smile.

"But I'm not always 'there'," I stammered, "I mean, home is where I'm not." My heat began to build. "You're always trying to excuse me!"

Margaret, forever the trusting wife, persisted. "But what you're doing at the church is so important."

"Don't! Don't say that! You just reinforce my foolishness."

"What foolishness?"

"I'm doing what Janet said you're doing with the kids. I'm letting the church run my life. I'm trapped, stuck, and don't know how to get out."

An east wind began to kick up waves on the river, and forced our little threesome to retreat. As our Plymouth rocked with the gustiness, I could almost read the silent thoughts running through my mate's mind. She would worry whether they were dressed warmly enough. Should she climb out of the car and help them change their play? She relaxed a bit when they began to build sand castles.

But I didn't relax. Our talk had led me toward the quicksands of our life, and I simply had to wade through with all my pain. "Maggie, so far we've only touched the edge of our problem. You know, I told you about Janet laying it on me about my 'wistful longing.' She hit me where it hurts worst. My loneliness. She didn't call it that. But that's what it is."

"Gosh, honey, how can you be lonely?" Margaret was all tenderness and disbelief. "We have each other."

I took a firm hold on my feelings and spoke as gently as I knew how. "What you haven't caught onto yet is that my sex needs are different from yours."

She didn't catch my direction. The old familiar refrain came up again. "By bedtime I'm so tired..."

I interrupted. "I'm not talking just about intercourse. What I'm trying to say is that I'm a touch person and you are not!"

"But we touch each other all the time."

"No, we don't! Sure, you give me a quick kiss now and then, but we don't take time to cuddle. You don't reach across the bed and lay a hand on me to let me know..."

"You keep telling me that," she said, "but I keep forgetting. I get so preoccupied with the children..."

My words failed for the moment, and then I plunged. "My touching you is ten to one over your touching me. Touch is the loudest way to say, 'I love you.'" I gulped. "Oh, it's not your fault! I've had to remind myself a dozen times that there isn't a coquettish bone in your body. I've got to let you be who you are."

She snuggled closer on the front seat, with the best of intentions, but she couldn't erase in that moment all the nights when I found my sleeping beauty sunk into her hundred-year-long coma.

"I've been thinking about this a lot, Margie." I stared absently through the windshield, down the river. "At last I see what I have to do: cut back on some of the big things I keep driving to achieve, pull in my shingle as a counselor. My number one job is to practice at home what I preach in the pulpit. Loving my family begins with spending time at home."

Margaret shook my arm to break my reverie. I saw light dawning in her face. "Yes! That's good. But it is my fault too. I have aided and abetted your over-conscientiousness. It's my pride in all the things you accomplish at the church." She lifted her face to mine. "No wonder we both suffer from over-work and fatigue."

I kissed her.

She took my hand firmly in hers and smiled a smile that warmed the whole interior of our Plymouth. "To have you home more would be a great lift for me. It might help both of us to get back on track."

I drew her closer. Certainly our Impossible Dream of helping the world must begin at home. Counsel yourself first, Mr. Would-Be-Therapist. Maybe that's why you haven't been able to make your helping hand for others really help.

The east wind blew away the foggy haze and gave us a beautiful clear blue sky as the sun dropped lower in the west. Margaret's head rested on my shoulder, the way it had on the bench at Lake Merritt. Love had come back to the Dimocks in a surprising visitation.

And then Mother Nature delivered a wonderful gift. As we sat rejoicing, the sound of chirping birds and flapping wings came strongly to us. Blackbirds flew overhead. Lots of them. We climbed out of the car to see more clearly. Close to us, barely twenty feet above, a river of birds fifty feet wide streamed westward down the island toward San Francisco Bay. Thousands of them flew noisily, swiftly, on a strange migration such as we had never imagined possible. The flight continued for more than five minutes, and then they were gone.

In awe and full of wonder Margaret and I hugged each other, and I felt to myself, "The black shadows of our life together have fled. What a marvelous way to find each other again."

Our effort to keep our bold resolutions succeeded somewhat better than those made conventionally at New Year's. I found more time to devote myself to the home scene and ease the load that Margaret had shouldered in solo fashion.

Soon we came to a sense of closure for our eight years at Antioch. We did not want to repeat the mistake we had made at Arlington and stay beyond what divine guidance was nudging us to do next. We were ready for a new calling and it came as we went exploring into the Northwest during our summer vacation.

Restless in Paradise
(1957-64)

As our family made the move to a new parish in Seattle, I found increasing joy in my marriage and in our children. But I was not prepared for a strange restlessness that soon began to seize Herb.

We arrived in West Seattle on a cloudy November day in 1957. The moving van disgorged our furnishings into the big, old-fashioned parsonage, and I enjoyed the adventure of rearranging and unpacking.

A few evenings later, however, Herb and I stood facing each other in our upstairs bedroom, listening in awed unbelief to the buckets of thunderous rain that pounded on the roof and dormer windows. Eight hundred miles north of our dear Antioch home, the unfamiliar surroundings and heavy rain suddenly overwhelmed me with a feeling of uprootedness. Herb seemed to share my feeling, for he asked, half-joking but half-serious, "What are we doing here, anyway?!"

Yet the move, like so many other changes in our life, seemed to have been guided by the "hand of God." Through the inexplicable delay of a letter from an Arizona church, which probably would have drawn us into service there, we had been steered to the Northwest instead!

Within a week or two, we began to feel at home. I loved our "mansion," with its spacious living room and four upstairs bedrooms, and its graceful birch trees on the front lawn. We lived only half a block from Puget Sound, a body of water that reminded me of our beloved San Francisco Bay, but with more grandeur. Beyond the Sound, to the west, lay the majestic snow-capped Olympic Mountains.

During the early months of Herb's preaching at Alki Congregational Church, he was able to repeat many of his best sermons from the past. This freed him to spend Saturdays taking the whole family on excursions to explore our new setting. Despite clouds and frequent drizzle, he pushed ahead in arranging for ferry boat rides and trips to museums, parks, zoo, and theaters.

But preaching was not his only obligation. For a decade, the local church leaders had felt that the old, dark-red brick building was no longer sufficient to meet the needs of the growing church and the burgeoning Sunday School.

By the time Herb and I arrived on the scene, plans had been drawn for an adjacent new sanctuary and social hall, and much of the funding had been provided for. There came a day when the Church Council approached their new pastor with urgency and hope: "Shall we now go ahead and sign the necessary contracts for construction?"

"Of course I had to say, 'By all means!'" Herb told me that night as we prepared for bed. "I could just see the wave of relief pass over their faces."

At first I thought he was bringing me good news. I was glad the Council had been impressed with his past success in building church edifices. But in response to my words of congratulation, Herb shrugged restlessly and complained, "Another building project is not what I'm really enthusiastic about."

However, he answered the call of duty. The beautiful new sanctuary was dedicated before the end of our first year, and the congregation and its officers were pleased.

In 1959, a history of the Alki Church written by one of the members, Elizabeth Rider Montgomery, gave words of praise for Herb's work.

> The Rev. Herbert Dimock, called from Antioch, California, soon proved to be a master organizer, a good executive in a very quiet way, adept at getting people to work, and a deeply spiritual person whose influence was soon felt throughout the church.
>
> With no apparent rush or great drive—with almost an appearance of hesitancy and frailty—he nevertheless accomplished a tremendous amount in a short space of time.

As for me, dwelling in the Alki parsonage brought a wonderful gift: opportunity for a quiet half-hour each morning, something I had never been able to pursue with any regularity since the advent of our children. Before anyone was up, or as soon as the family had left for school or church, I settled myself in a comfortable chair beside a window. With my back to the rest of the big living room, I had chosen this place as my special corner. On the wall in front of me hung a large picture of Jesus—a detail from Munkacsy's "Christ Before Pilate." It was a gift from Marrion Jones, an Antioch friend who had handed down to us so many material and artistic items that we had come to refer to her as our "fairy godmother." Beneath the picture, on a small round table, lay a Bible and several devotional books. Here I wrestled with problems, read, rejoiced, reflected and prayed. Often I put my thoughts and feelings in a notebook, under the title, "Morning Meditations."

Many entries were about our offspring, like this one:

Before retiring I made the rounds to see that the children were covered. I paused by each ones bed. Jonnie, who had been on a rugged weekend Scout trip, was sleeping so peacefully. I could see in his face similarities to the little one-year-old Jonnie whom I used to know, and my heart was lifted with wonder and love. How important it is to take time to savor our children—like holding jewels up to the light to exult over their beauty! How wrong we are to think of our children only in terms of discipline and schedules and irritation at the stubborn and immature things they do!...

And Larry, our dear bird-watcher—something like a little bird himself, bright-eyed and full of chirps and animal sounds that he likes to make.... And Martha... How she delights us with her creativeness, cheerfulness, gracefulness, femininity.

Some were about Herb:

I thank Thee, Lord, for this full rich week....

And how I love my dear husband! I don't know why I ever complain about anything—our mutual appreciation of each other is so very soul-gratifying!

But Herb did not have the peace I was finding, and he did complain. One noon I enjoyed preparing one of our favorites for lunch, avocado-and-grapefruit salad. As I set our plates on the dining room table, I glanced with satisfaction at the lovely wallpaper with its woodland scenes sketched in shades of green and at the ruffled white curtains gracing our windows.

When Herb came through the front door, he looked grim and worn. Showing no appreciation for our pleasant surroundings, he gave me a perfunctory greeting and sat down heavily. He started eating mechanically, as if his mind was elsewhere.

I was distressed. "What's the matter, honey? Is something wrong?"

After a moment he replied with vehemence, "I'm getting fed up with the routines of this job." He chewed a few bites and then spilled out his frustrations. "Week after week I have the chores of putting together the Sunday bulletin and writing up the weekly 'Messenger.' This morning I was called on to solve janitorial problems, and then to discuss potluck arrangements with the ladies. And hanging over my head is the necessity to plan soon for the Every Member Canvass for pledges. Always these repetitive, uninspiring duties!"

I listened patiently, trying to understand his discontentedness.

"I'm an innovator!" he finally burst out. "I don't thrive on routine."

"But Herb," I protested, "we've been saying for years that we have to have organized institutions as well as innovation. Human society couldn't survive without both!"

"I know, I know," he conceded. "But maintaining a smoothly functioning religious organization just doesn't fulfil my sense of destiny!"

I sympathized with his discomfort, but all I could do was write in my Meditations notebook, "I pray with all my heart, Lord, for Thy light and joy to bless him."

A source of redeeming light did come quite soon. Herb was invited to visit a "Yokefellow" group that several West Seattle ministers had started. It reminded him of our fruitful experiences with prayer groups in Kensington and Antioch, and he and I agreed to start a similar group in our own church.

The dozen or so women who joined us every Wednesday morning in the new church parlor gradually became a close-knit fellowship. We shared our individual failings in carrying out the daily readings and prayer time we had committed ourselves to, or in living up to the ideals we talked about so enthusiastically. We rejoiced together when any one of us could report a small triumph in spiritual growth. Herb and I both found the Sunday worship services more meaningful because we were aware of these spiritually-alive "yokefellows" scattered through the congregation.

Yet Herb often came down with periods of illness, such as sinus infections. I reported on one such episode in my Meditations notebook:

After dragging along with fatigue and discomfort for 3 weeks or so, Herb suddenly was healed inwardly Sunday afternoon as he gave up resentments at not having had a real vacation and having too much to do. Amazingly the fatigue disappeared and the nasal passages cleared up. For two glorious days he was full of serenity and joyousness—as You meant him to be—while carrying a full load.

That period of joy did not last. But eventually a new kind of joy began to blossom as Herb discovered rich opportunities for drama.

Beyond writing a Christmas play about St. Francis and the first creche, he created a five-episode story of "Johanan ben Arni," a fictional disciple of Jesus in the first century. In costume he presented this as a monologue at junior high camp as well as at our Sunday School, and the young folks loved it. The buried playwright in his soul had come to life, and with great eagerness he plunged into several Biblical one-act plays. I was entranced with the way he made the old stories of Abraham and Lot, of Isaiah and King Hezekiah, and of Cain and Abel come alive with meaning for contemporary life. Although these never got performed on stage, Herb found the writing amply satisfying.

Then a surprising development thrust him into a spot where his dramatic talent could have wider influence. He was elected to the Conference Evangelism Committee, and became its chairman. This put him on the Conference Board of Directors.

"The church needs to dramatize its message!" he insisted over and over to the Board members. They caught his vision and urged him to act on it. He did.

His finest moment came when his dramatic skit, "Judgment at Spokane," was performed, by players he had chosen and directed, at the Annual Conference as it met in that city. The play was a clever evaluation of church lacks, as well as achievements, in the form of a court hearing. I could feel the audience overflowing with warm response and joy as I sat among them. Afterwards, I stood beside Herb while congratulatory crowds deluged him with accolades.

At Alki I had abundant scope for my own creative activity. Never really at ease in teaching children, I gladly agreed to teach an adult Sunday School class. No behavior problems there! I found it exhilarating to discuss with this responsive group the life of Jesus and other sections of the Bible. In the Woman's Fellowship I formed vital friendships. I even relished fixing myself up with earrings and lipstick and permanent waves like the rest; having given up my earlier attitudes of scorn, I had come to see these conventions as a means of affirming my solidarity with other women. Study groups, choir, the local PTA—all filled my days with stimulating challenges.

Unexpectedly, Mary Zoe came to live with our family, and this became the biggest challenge of all—for both Herb and me. A pupil in our Sunday School, Mary Zoe was also a neighborhood playmate of Martha's, with whom she often walked to school. When she arrived in the morning, she sometimes had had no breakfast, and we shared our food with her. Day after day I noticed that her jacket remained torn and dirty. She dropped hints about the violent fights between her mother and step-father, especially when they had been drinking. One day she told us her mother had taken sleeping pills and fallen asleep while smoking, and the mattress caught fire. Finally her family fell apart in a crisis so severe as to require intervention by the Juvenile Court, and Mary Zoe became a resident at the Youth Center.

Herb attended the preliminary hearing, and telephoned me from the court. "The judge wants to know if we'll be a temporary foster home for Mary Zoe," he said, after explaining the situation.

I had long felt distress over Mary Zoe's lack of normal parental care, and now I sensed Divine Providence at work in presenting us with an opportunity to be a part of this wistful little girl's life.

"Oh, yes!" I answered Herb. "Anything, to give whatever love and hope we can. Don't you agree?"

"Definitely! I just wanted to be sure *you* did."

For me, taking on Mary Zoe at age nine was almost like having another baby: fascinating and rewarding, though also time-consuming and wearing.

She was an appealing child, only a year younger than Martha, with a sweet singing voice and a flair for art work. But she had lots of dark memories that came out in horrible nightmares. She complained that she was "stupid" and that the other kids didn't like her. In anger, she threw pencils and a hairbrush around the bedroom. Once she packed clothing into a pillowcase and started to "run away."

Yet the wonderful thing about Mary Zoe was that she wanted to grow. With stuffed animals and bedtime lullabies, little songs and stories, hugs and pats, I poured in the kind of nurturing I felt she had missed in her babyhood. She lapped it up. When Herb was around, he too did his best to give her encouragement and guidance. At first somewhat fearful about relating to men, she gradually warmed up to him. We both rejoiced when her fears and frustrations diminished.

After many months, the Juvenile Court worker told us that the home situation of the mother and step-father seemed to have stabilized to the point that Mary Zoe could soon return to them. She had several weekend visits to that home, and then confided with trembling lip, "Sometimes I want to go back to my parents and sometimes I don't. I feel safer here."

As the date for the court's decision grew closer, Mary Zoe still felt uncertain and scared. Sitting on the edge of her bed, I told her earnestly, "Mary Zoe, whichever way the court decides, we will still be your friends, and love you, and hope and pray for the very best for you always."

Her answer was profoundly touching: "You're so wonderful! You're sorta like a mother and sorta like a counselor and sorta like a guardian—and sometimes I think of you as a second-hand God."

Although the court did decree a return to her parents, I knew that, one way or another, she would continue to be a part of our hearts and lives.

Even during the time we were centrally absorbed in helping Mary Zoe find a measure of peace and security in her life, Herb and I also became acutely uneasy about the lack of peace in the wider world. News reports came constantly of trouble spots in Africa, unrest in Israel, controversy over West Berlin, belligerence from Red China, uncertainty about Cuba. Most of all, we shuddered at the escalating nuclear arms race between the Soviet Union and our own land.

I looked across the choppy waters of the Sound to where the Olympic Mountains rose in solid splendor, and thought with a shock, "If a third World War does break out, all this magnificent beauty will be destroyed!"

We received a two-page letter from the Seattle school administration detailing how evacuation from school buildings would be carried out in case of "threatened enemy attack." Our kids had to wear identification bracelets on their wrists. At school, during civil defense drills, they were taught to dive under their desks.

My usual daily cheerfulness sagged into sadness. At lunch one day I lamented to Herb, "Once an atomic war starts, I don't see how it could ever be stopped!"

He looked up from his vegetable soup, and surprised me with a surge of optimism. "I've been groping for some action we could take to prevent that from happening," he said. "I think I now have a clue. I see where the power to change things lies."

My spirits brightened at my creative husband's confident statement. Yet I wondered what he meant. "Where does it lie?" I asked expectantly.

"In small groups!" he almost shouted. "Small face-to-face groups. Like our prayer groups, and Yokefellow groups. Like your Bible classes, my teachers' meetings, and the groups that inspired us long ago at Camp Farthest Out. That's where the power of the New Society is to be found."

I was confused by his terminology. I always thought "New Society" meant some kind of economic system. But in the months that followed, the meaning of what he was talking about began to dawn on me.

The radiant daylight of understanding filled my soul when, in the summer of 1962, Herb came home from a solitary "study-and-writing retreat." Friends had let him use their rustic cabin on Whidbey Island, in Puget Sound, where he stayed for three weeks.

On his return, I could see the ecstasy in his face as he entered the front door of our Alki parsonage. I longed to hear what had happened to him, but reunion with the children and the routines of dinner claimed first attention.

As soon as other family activities had quieted down, Herb and I withdrew to our room. We sat on the edge of our carved walnut bed, and he began his story. "I had intended to work on my new play, but something else took over. As I walked back and forth along the shore, these ideas about the New Society and the Old Society kept flooding into my consciousness. I went back into the cabin and wrote and wrote."

I pushed pillows against the headboard, and curled up comfortably to hear more. Herb drew his legs up onto the bed and faced me eagerly.

"This is a big thing that's grabbed me," he burst out. "For the first time in my intellectual questing, I see everything falling together in a grand pattern."

He went on to tell how clearly he saw the whole scene. The Old Society, he said, is made up of "institutions," accepted ways of doing things. Schools, churches, governments, business—all are organized in certain ways. They have rules, customs, traditions. These institutions are necessary and useful. But as they wield their power, they tend to become exclusive, rigid, and self-perpetuating, and they often ignore the needs of persons. In contrast, the New Society, which is to be found best in small face-to-face groups, can be inclusive and loving, flexible, forgiving, and sensitive to changing human needs. The only way the big institutions of society—including war—can be changed, is by the New Society's constant action to penetrate and influence the Old.

"How I love this guy," I thought as I listened, "especially when he is on fire with new ideas and determination!"

With shining eyes he continued. "I went through the New Testament to see what it had to say about this. It's amazing. Every page, almost every paragraph, makes more sense when you see it from this point of view."

He gave examples: The "Kingdom of Heaven" is another name for the New Society! When Jesus spoke of the Kingdom as being like leaven, or yeast, hidden in a lump of dough, he was giving a picture of how small groups of New Society people can work with gentle, irresistible power to lift the Old Society out of its heavy condition of selfishness and greed.

The Pharisees, who opposed Jesus, were stuck in the rigidity of the Old Society. Paul was describing the New Society when he told a group of new Christians that they were to be like various organs of the human body, accepting their different functions, and not presuming one was more important than another. And on and on.

"I felt as though I was standing on the growing edge of creation," Herb exulted, "and looking at the wonder of the divine design and destiny the Creator has for us."

I was overcome with the joy of being with him as he shared his vision. "That's beautiful," I said.

But then a chill of realism blew through my mind. "How will this new outlook of yours prevent nuclear war?" I asked anxiously. "If you preach it in our own church, or even in all the churches of Seattle, can it make a difference to enough people soon enough? I mean, in time to stop the frightful descent of our whole world into complete devastation?"

Herb nodded with a knowing glint in his eye. "I've wrestled with that too! I want to touch thousands of people, even millions, and wake them up. So— I'm going to write a book. A novel!" He sketched the plot. He would tell of small pockets of survivors after a full-scale nuclear war, and how the characters learn from the disaster to pick up on New Society ways of living.

I was totally confident that he could do it. Hadn't he written wonderful plays? "That sounds marvelous!" I said. "And the hope is that your readers will be motivated to live as part of the New Society *now*, not holding back until after a tragic disaster. Right?"

He beamed his joy that I had caught on. We slipped off the bed and stood up, then hugged each other in passionate delight. I felt as if I "stood on the edge of creation" along with him. And when he said, "Margaret, I feel the time has come for us to embark on a new adventure," I was ready to follow wherever that led us.

At first the adventure took the form of efforts to write the novel. During what was left of the summer, Herb started making notes and outlines. I gloried in being a back-board for his ideas.

All too soon, responsibilities for the fall program of the church were upon him, and time for the book dwindled. But he had made a beginning! And for many months his insights into the New Society integrated all his preaching and thinking. I saw him more full of joy than he had been in years.

Then Herb's mother, "Grandma," came to live with us! It was no longer wise for her, at eighty-eight, to live alone in her Los Angeles apartment. Her landlord called us long-distance to tell how he worried over the careless way she crossed a traffic-filled street in the middle of the block. Herb and I agreed that the time had come for us to have her in our home. She resisted the suggestion strongly, but finally gave in to Herb's insistent urging.

I had managed to endure Grandma's criticisms and complaints during the twice-yearly visits she made to Seattle by Greyhound bus. But I soon found that having her with us full time was no simple matter. Her verbal attacks on Herb had essentially disappeared; and she basked in the respect and honor our church people gave her as "the minister's mother." She clashed with me, however, on many fronts.

She wanted me available every minute. "Why didn't you tell me you were going upstairs?"

She gave her opinions sharply. "Margaret! You shouldn't let Larry have such a large helping of cranberry sauce!"

Mournfully, "Nobody will play with Grandma."

She was quick to feel rejected and jealous, and in return I felt annoyed and resentful. There were crises when I "blew my lid," and angry words leaped out of my mouth beyond my control. Such episodes left me physically trembling. When I cried on Herb's shoulder afterward, he was always able to give me comfort and perspective.

"Pretend we're workers in a mental hospital," he advised. "She's an immature, neurotic patient. Let's see how we can relate to her on New Society principles."

I knew what he meant. Our treating her in a loving way was one kind of peace-making for the world.

I did struggle hard to accept and forgive. Gradually I was more often able to let go of my habits of irritation and defensiveness, and find a creative solution to our differences. When I put my attention on her good qualities, like her alertness and inner vitality, and her writing of poetry, my changed attitude helped her change too. Her attendance at the Yokefellow group every week helped both of us understand and forgive each other. "Sometimes I even *like* her!" I told Herb in surprise.

But no matter how much we tried to make things pleasant for her, she never seemed quite happy. She had frequent moods of melancholy. In my "Morning Meditations" notebook I commented sadly on "Grandma's small capacity to enjoy," and, in contrast, I bubbled over with my own joys:

> Life is just full of opportunities to enjoy, and I do! I enjoy food, and sleep, and sex, and clouds and music and dancing and all forms of beauty, and motherhood and responsibility and challenge and reading and memories and housework and serving in the church and poetry—endless things.

By the fall of 1963, Herb's joy over his big dream of saving the world through his novel was tainted by frustration. He'd been at the writing for more than a year, mostly "in between times," and progress lagged. On our twenty-fourth wedding anniversary, we stayed awake late into the night with much soul-searching.

"I don't sleep well, and I feel tired all the time," Herb grumbled. "And I'm anxious about the church. Attendance and membership are lower than last year at this time. And the finances are shaky."

I laid my hand on his arm in sympathy.

He tossed and turned, and agonized, "Most of all I feel this great pressure from within to *write*, and I'm not getting any time for it." He was quiet for a minute or two, and then raised a big question. "Should I maybe leave the parish ministry for awhile? But then how would we support the family?"

I didn't know what to say. In my notebook I recorded my bewilderment:

> I sense his feelings so keenly that I too get a little depressed. And then
> I'm not much help to him.... O Lord, what wouldst Thou have?

In November Herb was all set to undertake a new discipline: to spend one hour every morning at writing "O My God!—The Diary of a Survivor" before he got involved in church obligations. We even bought a special table, second-hand, so he could write at home in our bedroom. He sat down at the new table on November 22, ready to work.

That day, I drove to the West Seattle shopping area to do errands. In the Kress variety store, I heard a staggering radio announcement: President Kennedy had been shot! I ran across the street to a phone booth and called Herb.

That was the end of his writing. Kennedy's death, TV coverage, and special church services absorbed his attention for several days, as we mourned with the rest of our countrymen. Then came the Christmas season with its busy activities.

From time to time Herb brought up the subject of his book. He told me that two of our church laymen had taken a great interest in it, and one of them encouraged him to send the first 160 pages to a publisher in San Francisco. "If the publisher shows solid interest in it," Herb said to me the day he mailed it, "maybe I could ask for a three-month leave of absence this summer, to finish it."

The manuscript's return with a letter of rejection was only briefly dampening to Herb. There were other publishers.

But one night in March as we prepared for bed, he said, "I've decided three months won't be enough. Besides, Maggie, my heart is really not here in the institutional church. I'll just have to resign, and leave."

I was not too surprised at this development. But now that it had been spoken, I began to realize what great changes were in the air. Where would we live? Where would the money come from? Would Herb's story ideas continue to flow as they had so far? Many unknowns!

Actually, I would have been content to stay at Alki indefinitely, but certainly not if Herb felt called to some greater path. I had strong faith, with a big mixture of naivete and romanticism, that God would be with us in the way ahead.

As we plunged into bed, Herb exploded with the final word: "There's no doubt about it, darling. We're through!" And I snuggled up against him in complete agreement.

Our Bold Leap
(1964-74)

I don't know when Joseph Campbell formulated his great commandment that we should "follow our bliss," but 1964, for me, was the hour. Now or never! It turned out to be Margaret's bliss also. But we found quite soon that to follow one's bliss does not mean that the road won't be bumpy. What it does mean is that you are doing from day to day what is deepest in your heart to do.

My uneasiness about the parish ministry, which grew ever larger during our Alki years, was only made tolerable by my day-to-day contentment with our marriage. I could count on Margaret, she could count on me, in the fulfilling of daily chores, home care, job, raising of children, coping with mother-in-law. In a way "conventional" was the word to describe us. And then everything changed: career and marriage and our vision of the future.

In April I announced my resignation to the congregation to take effect at the end of July. Financially that meant we had to scramble. We sat down as eager plotters with pencil and paper, and went to work on the best plan we could dream up.

"We have the savings account that Fairy Godmother Jones set up for us," I said with my pulse stepping up.

"But that's only a thousand dollars," Margaret protested. "It would last us three months, at the very best."

"Not good enough." I had to agree as Margaret, the family bookkeeper, went on to recite our expenses for Jon at Dartmouth College, Larry a high school senior and Martha in junior high, and Grandma to care for. But as she talked I sensed a sparking in her imagination.

"You know," she began, "with the kids older, I have a lot more discretionary time." She hesitated. "With your being at home, I might go back to my social work. What do you think?"

I had not thought that her long dormant career was something she would want to return to, but as soon as she brought it out of the closet I grabbed it as our answer. I encouraged her to explore the possibilities, and with each succeeding week I saw her excitement increase. By the middle of May she had won a job with the State of Washington to begin July 1st.

The entry pay was only $420 per month, and that was still not enough, along with savings, to cover our budget even for one year.

Was this folly? Were we mad to abandon the major security I enjoyed at the top of my ministerial career? Yes, certainly we were crazy, but our venture into the unknown was something we simply had to do. It was our bliss! For Margaret it was a chance to escape the home duty of care for her mother-in-law, and for me, a chance to write.

The search for our first non-parsonage home led us to a long-term blessing. For a rent of only $110 per month we acquired four bedrooms in a handsome two-story white shiplap house on Belvidere Avenue. It was on the east side of West Seattle, perched high on the bluff. We had a panoramic view of Seattle's industrial district, and on clear days a vision of Mt. Rainier off to the southeast.

The discipline of our daily lives changed dramatically. Margaret took the bus each morning to the King County Hospital, into a new world of patients and doctors and lawyers. I became the homebody, fixing meals, washing dishes, doing the laundry, and then hustling to my writing desk where I put in six hours a day pounding out my novel, "O My God!" The new regime had a marvelous effect on my health. In six months I added fifteen pounds to my skinny one hundred fifty. Also there developed a wonderful change in my relationship with Mother Martha Yale. She and I enjoyed lunchtime together, and for the first time since 1939 there was no dominating criticism. She was happier than I had ever known her to be. She was supremely content with the lives we all were leading.

"I know this is silly," I confessed to Margaret one day in late September as I met her at her bus stop, "but I feel guilty about not earning any money. I can't shake the feeling that I'm failing my responsibility as a breadwinner." It was a return of that old, old message the culture had laid on me about males being the head of the household.

Margaret protested vigorously. "But it's my turn now! We always said it didn't matter whether you or I earned the money, as long as we were doing something worthwhile. But you know what? I find that getting paid for work gives me a feeling of elevated status."

With that I kept my silence. Something new had entered our relationship. Margaret knew it and tried to give big support for my half of the bargain.

"Besides," she said, squeeezing my arm as we walked home, "when your book is published it will bring in important income."

The days opened one upon another, and I discovered that there was huge naivete in her image of what I was accomplishing, and also naivete in my readiness to go along with her estimate. There would be no dollars rolling in, because, as it turned out, I was not writing a salable book. Instead, I was learning some of the hard lessons about how to become a writer, how to tell a story. I found it wise to join a writers' class to test my work on others who were struggling with the same challenges. I also assembled my first collection of rejection slips as I submitted partial manuscripts. But worst of all, the world, for which I wrote my horror story about the atomic threat, was changing faster than my plot. The great opus, "O My God!", was finished in six months and found an uneasy place on the shelf.

And then we ran out of money, and I had to search for new options. My first part-time assignment was to be interim pastor for the Beacon Hill Congregational Church. The task was to help a dying institution, which had only three or four dozen elderly members, to merge with the Olivet Church about two miles to the south. I had to practice sensitive diplomacy; give repeated assurances that this "death" would be followed by a wonderful resurrection. We took almost three years to accomplish the transition, and at last there emerged a new entity: the Beacon Avenue United Church of Christ. They paid me fifty dollars a week for my work, and that helped to keep our family ship afloat.

In the midst of that time, in November of '65, our beloved Mary Zoe came to live with us permanently. All our labor with her natural family ended in futility, and the court determined that she must be relinquished by her mother or become a lost soul. She was not a financial burden, because Social Service provided foster care expense money. I was glad to be the available parent. When she came home from junior high each day I was able to comfort and counsel her, and I rejoiced to watch a steady growth out of her emotional hell.

In the midst of 1967 divine wisdom made it necessary for us to purchase our rental house, which had been put up for sale, or scramble to move to some new location. We chose to burden ourselves with a mortgage that boosted our rent to only $115 a month. It turned out to be the best investment we ever made, for the following inflationary years increased its value from fifteen thousand to thirty-five thousand dollars.

After my Beacon Avenue stint, our new pattern of life made another shift. Larry, now a student at the University of Washington, was the catalyst. "Dad," he said to me, "I have been attending group meetings at the First Avenue Service Center. I think you'd be interested in what they're trying to do."

The Center had been started over a year before, to provide a meeting place for Skid Road "street people," an alternative to the religious missions that were ready to feed and house them in exchange for saving their souls.

I went with Larry several times, enough to get hooked and to volunteer to be their publicity agent. Then Larry left. I stayed.

The Seattle Times honored me with my first published article: "From the Fringe to the Center." It also became a chapter in a book put out by Pilgrim Press titled, "Creative Ministries." In it I wrote:

The swinging doors screech as you come in off the street. To the eye of a suburbanite the appearance of the inside is no more promising than the outside. Ragtag davenports line the walls, a TV chatters mindlessly, coarse men cluster around a couple of pinochle games, the air is blue with cigarette smoke. But there is also the aroma of coffee, the business-like whir of a washing machine, and the noise of sharp clicks as young people bat out a game of table tennis. Then there is the friendly inquiry of a person who seems to be shouldering responsibility, "Can I help you?"

The volunteers who spoke those words might be people from suburbia: a housewife, a business man, an electronics engineer, a college student. Or they might be a prostitute, a hippie, an ex-convict, a drug user. They shared one purpose. They wanted to help the outcasts of Seattle escape the fragmented, lonely, estranged existence that was the common denominator of all. They wanted to create a new community.

I think it was the pain of the street that pulled me. Margaret and I, in the beginning of our marriage, had talked deeply about serving the down-and-outers of society. But with the exception of our summer in Cope, our assignment had been to the successful, comfortable middle class. Now I came face to face with the homeless, the jobless, the powerless; men and women in the never-never land of despair; the winos, the scavengers in the garbage cans of First Avenue, people who had nothing and no one to live for,

That was the thing that kindled a fire in my solar plexus. I began to write in support of something I deeply believed in, a cause "out in the world," a different kind of "parish" ministry. And I was being published: in the Seattle Times, in the United Church Herald, in local weekly church newsletters. And at last, about a year after my beginning, the Northwest Writers Conference awarded me first prize for an article I had produced about the Center. Margaret always heartily applauded my achievements.

At this same time Margaret was struggling with her new AFDC caseload (Aid to Families with Dependent Children). Although she had at first said, "It's even more fascinating than my work at the hospital," she soon found it much more difficult. And in August of '67, while I was feeling new excitement over how I might help the people of Skid Road, Margaret skidded down to her nadir.

"I'm so terribly inadequate and inefficient," she mourned, as I drove our red station wagon across the Olympic Peninsula toward the Pacific Ocean.

We had eagerly arranged for this vacation camping trip, but Margaret was exhausted from several days of overtime to catch up on paper work at her office. In tears she poured out her woe. "I'm always spending time on the wrong things. I just can't hack it. I feel as bad as if I'd been fired."

Through the years I had learned that her tears were rarely the harbinger of real disaster, and so I listened with all patience. Finally, as we drew into a campsite, she gave a sigh of self-discovery. "The humiliation is painful, but I needed it. I've been arrogant and egotistical, assuming that of course I'm a good social worker. I'm not."

I put my arm around her, and gave what comfort I could. "You'll feel better about all that after you're rested."

She slept soundly that night. The next day we wandered at our leisure along the wild coast at Rialto Beach. The weather was perfect, the rhythm of the breakers soothing, and I watched with relief as Margaret's discouragement drained away. She was able to smile at last. "I can face life again," she said. "And thanks for everything."

A month later she reported, "My supervisor's evaluation rated my performance 'satisfactory.' I must be doing something right." The following spring she was invited to switch to a caseload of children in foster homes, which was to prove the richest and most satisfying experience of all.

But for both of us the satisfaction of helping poverty people was shadowed by the growing terror of America's undeclared war in Vietnam. We shared the rising protest that cried for the end of that insanity. We also wept for the assassinations of Martin Luther King and Bobby Kennedy.

And then a jolting crisis hit the First Avenue Service Center, where my best efforts as a volunteer were focused on producing a film story about the need and the work. The date was December 9, 1968. The acting director suffered what everyone referred to euphemistically as a nervous breakdown. I first heard about it when the chairman of the Board of Directors called me on the phone and asked the big question. "Herb, would you be willing to take over the director's job, to get us through the holidays?"

I phoned Margaret at her office and described the need. Her first reaction came out of our romantic idealism, with a lighthearted excitement that I had met so many times before. "That's what we've always wanted, isn't it? You could really do a job!"

Her second thoughts dealt with a couple of pieces of reality, also the way she always responded to any of my big ideas. "Would that mean we'd have to hire a sitter for Grandma? And what about another car? We'd each need one."

I took the job at the Center, but failed to pin down the chairman of the Board as to which holidays he had in mind. That was the effective end of my writing career for more than two and a half years.

It was one thing to be on the fringe of the First Avenue Service Center community, looking in as suburbanite, and quite another to be at the center of the Center, the primary leader. I did not, at the beginning, have the credentials. I did not have the charisma of my predecessor. I was an outsider. Every night I left the Avenue for my home and family and a hot supper, while the homeless people in their abysmal poverty made out in whatever way they could—sleeping "under the bridge" or in one of the missions or a flop house or the "Dirty Bird," which was the name they gave to the flea-infested Green Parrot Moviehouse.

Just before Christmas the worst snowstorm in years hit Seattle and piled up drifts that lasted more than a month. For Skid Road people it was a catastrophe. There were not enough beds to escape to during the night. When the police checked the sleepers "under the bridge" they found five men, covered with newspapers, frozen, dead. As the grapevine spread the word, feelings of anger and despair swept the Center. The survivors knew that any one of them could have been the unlucky ones who had no bed. They were furious that the larger community didn't care, didn't even take note in the daily papers.

January 1969 passed and, since the Board had not found a new director, I settled into my new role. Again I was earning an income. For the first time both Margaret and I had full-time jobs, both social workers, with salaries almost the same, about $800 per month. We joked about our affluence, how we were "getting rich"!

The Center also was growing, not financially, but in popularity with the street people. I realized that we needed bigger quarters, so I maneuvered new rental space in a former basement-saloon at the corner of Seneca and First. It was huge, and featured a long bar along one wall. The labor of moving and re-shaping our program was equally huge.

Workaholic? For sure! All over again!

To help with the growing work load, I hired an assistant, Jim, to serve as floor manager. In a letter adddressed to son Larry, now at Harvard Divinity School, I made the following estimate of my lead helper.

> I puzzle about Jim. His Irish-type drinking in the past has been a serious obstacle to effective work in any system. But there is no question about his ability: sharp mind, smooth tongue, and gravelly voice team up to command attention. Two years of college helped. Time in prison roughened him. There is a touch of policeman in his manner. But also he comes on as a natural social worker.

The struggles of the summer of '69 included some heart-wrenching developments at home. Mother was approaching her ninety-fifth birthday and finding it more and more difficult to cope with her aging. At last we had to provide nursing home care just a few blocks from our Belvidere place.

Late one night the phone rang and the nurse told us that Mother had called her to bedside and had said quite calmly, "I think I'm going to die." As the nurse put her arms around Mother, death came quietly as she had forseen.

I led a memorial service back at Alki Church, in which I read many of her excellent pieces of poetry. Margaret and I were glad that I could end our long struggle with a positive tribute to her amazing creative personality. Yet in the days that followed I had the gnawing awareness that there was still some unfinished business between Mother and me, and I didn't know how to cope with it.

During the fall of '69, in spite of all the successes our staff and volunteers had with the people, the Center ran out of money. The treasurer couldn't afford to pay my salary. He could only eke out the rent, Jim's stipend, and the insurance.

But an answer to our need for dollars came through a succession of amazing events. In the beginning, the anger of the Center community over last winter's deaths by freezing was reawakened. Following Thanksgiving, men crowded in, bitter and hostile, ready for violence. I encouraged Jim to be their spokesman. We tried to open channels with city and county officialdom and got the usual run-around. Our angry mob was ready to burn the boxcars they were forced to sleep in. Jim cooled them with promise of real action.

The next day the Cause came fully to birth. The men held a march to City Hall. Each guy held a piece of typing paper with a demand: We Want Jobs, We Want Food, We Want Housing. More than two hundred strong they marched through the heart of the city, fourteen blocks to the place of power. They caught the police completely off guard and shook up the Establishment.

The Mayor, protesting that the city had no funds, acted to provide two buses for our ragtaggers and sent the protestors the next day to the State Capitol in Olympia to confront the Governor. He was conveniently "out of town," so our people met with the head of the Welfare Department. He sent them back to Seattle with the promise of relief, under "exception to policy." Housing was provided. Food vouchers granted.

The media picked up the story, and the "revolution" began to happen. Citizens all over the city heard about the First Avenue Service Center and were moved by the crisis, and by the Christmas spirit, to mail in checks and currency from one dollar on up. I wrote to Larry:

> People stopped in the front office and left money anonymously. One giver sold some stock through Merrill Lynch, and I was instructed to come and pick up the proceeds—$2300. A grand total of $4700 was given for the emergency in just a couple of days. Also our campaign for operating funds picked up steam. A VIP Appeal alone brought in more than $5000. So we're in very good shape....
> Love, Dad

We had lots of negotiating to do with the Establishment in Olympia and in the local offices, but the ice jam had been broken. I put together a team of lobbyists who kept up the pressure. Slowly big things began to develop, steady money for housing and food and counseling and jobs. It was a great turning point for the Center and for Skid Road.

But the toll on my health proved severe. Burn out. In February for a couple of weeks I was physically and spiritually sicker than I had been since my 1946 encounter with hepatitis. If it hadn't been for Margaret, I could have "gone under." She took some vacation time. We holed up in a cabin, again on Whidbey Island, offered by a college roommate of Marti's. I indulged in some real tears, ran a spanking good temperature, wrestled with chills and night-mares and depression.

Very soon I resigned as director, a new leader was found, and Margaret and I vowed to do some real vacationing. We roamed far and wide, to Idaho and Yellowstone and the wonders of Utah's magnificent scarps and canyons, and to our favorite Olympic beaches.

My next job, after the Center, took me into the halls of academia. At the Seattle campus of the Tacoma-based University of Puget Sound, I became the Adjunct Professor of Religion and Ethics. It was a School of Business and Public Administration, and all of my students were working-people questing for a master's degree that would move them up the professional ladder.

Suddenly a new thrill grabbed my soul. I was moving into Big Time. The academic quarter of nine weeks beginning January '72 launched my maiden voyage. I prepared with intense absorption to teach my first course: "Religion and Modern Man: the Old Testament." The school was still groping for class-room rental space, and therefore, at first, I had to meet my students in a brief-ing room in the City's Administration Building.

I reported to Margaret at suppertime. "You'll never believe what I went through this afternoon. My first class came trooping in by twos and threes, most of them policemen, twenty-five strong, and they had their artillery still strapped to their sides! My throat went dry. They were the guys who were on the opposite side of the battle line when I was on Skid Road!"

"What a wonderful opportunity," Margaret exulted. "Maybe you can get under their skin."

"Sure. But I've got to get over my reflexive awe that they represent the frontline of Authority in society."

"Why not! You represent the frontline Authority of the Church. You are the 'Man of God'!" That was my Margie all over again. Her humor came through unerringly.

As one term followed another, my portfolio of teaching expanded until I was handling three courses each quarter. I was having the most satisfying time of my whole professional career. In my second year the dean of the school asked me to teach a pioneering course: "Ethics and Values in Management." What? Ethics for politicians and government bureaucrats and corporate managers? In the early '70s there was perhaps one other school in the country that had experimented with this addition to the curriculum.

I was stirred, but also daunted. I wasn't sure that I knew enough. The design of the course called for the students to read a book a week for each of the nine weeks of the quarter, and I was to lead the class discussion.

My new course was nicknamed "Managerial Seminar," and the students proposed "B.S. 101." My initial meeting with them proved extraordinary, for I found the Seattle Chief of Police and two of his top lieutenants included in my list of enrollees. For two hours we talked and talked and talked, and my anxieties evaporated. I found the group enthralled with our discussion. My one objective was to help bureaucrats see the importance of humanizing their work, to help them purge out of their thinking and behavior the superior professional attitude that set them above the public they had to deal with. It was a course in the loving use of power.

At the end of the quarter the Chief honored me, saying, "At the beginning I was very skeptical that anything significant would come out of the class. You have convinced me. I will encourage all of my staff to enroll."

But even with those words of praise, I looked hard at the world we had inherited and found a deepening unease. Margaret and I had spent our working years trying to turn it into a better place, yet the scene seemed worse than ever. We knew in our hearts it was time for another phase of our bold leap. In the summer of '74 we followed our hearts back to sunny California and bought two acres in the Sierra Nevada foothills near Grass Valley. Our dream was that we could create a refuge to which people might escape from the collapsing cities.

Hand in hand Margaret and I stepped into the unknown future of our "retirement" with stars in our eyes and the reborn frontier spirit of our youth.

Doormat Strikes Back
(1974-1979)

When Herb and I bought the land near Grass Valley for our retirement locale, I certainly never realized what a radically new stage of our life together we had launched. I was focused on an idyllic image of escape from employment duties and city living to a Shangri-la in the country.

During the two years before my sixtieth birthday, I found my work in the state's child welfare program very tiring. It was as fascinating as ever, but the tragic morasses my clients were trapped in, and the difficult decisions I had to make, wore me down emotionally. I looked forward ardently to living in a quiet "hermitage," where we would keep healthy by working outdoors as we raised our own vegetables and fruits. There I would have time for nurturing my spirit, and for finishing my book on Auntie Laura, "Large Love from Laura Jane."

While I plugged away at my job, Herb was greatly enjoying his teaching at the University of Puget Sound—"more than I ever enjoyed my work as a parish minister," he told me. He also was happy with the vacation time available to him between quarters. Every chance he got during his breaks, he devoted himself to his new enthusiasm: developing our site at "Anathoth," as we had named our land. He drew plans for our future house and garden. He made his way to Anathoth by train, bus, or car, and did surveying, arranged for a well to be drilled, dug ditches for water-lines with a borrowed back-hoe and laid white plastic pipes in them.

"Is there anything this husband of mine doesn't know how to do?" I marvelled to myself as I viewed the snapshots of our velvet-green land that he brought home. I was glad to see him so integrated and joyful.

My chance to join him in this activity came in September of 1975. Making our headquarters in the home that my sister Lois and her husband Harry had recently built in that area, we drove ten miles to Anathoth every day, and in the course of three weeks made thrilling progress. I helped Herb mix concrete, build a wooden shed to house a pressure tank, and then paint its exterior green. Together we fashioned a protection for the well-head, and watched with amazement while a submersible pump was installed. We fixed gateposts at the entrance to the graveled driveway which the grading contractor had completed for us. I was perfectly content to follow along as assistant to Herb, for he knew more about all those things than I did.

Then, on the day before we were to start back to Seattle, a crisis hit us smack in the face. It started as a pleasant surprise. Herb said to me, "Why don't you take over the job of putting insulation around the faucet risers, so that when winter comes they won't freeze?" I agreed whole-heartedly, and he left for another project.

I found it keenly satisfying to be given a responsibility to carry out on my own. Taking the materials he had provided, I went off to my first riser. I figured out what I thought was a good way to apply the fiberglass insulation and fasten a plastic covering over it, and set to work. This was going to be fun!

But ten minutes later, Herb stood looking over my shoulder. "Now, that's not the way to do it," he said authoritatively. "Let me show you."

The dormant tiger within me rose up in protest, and I exploded with angry tears. I screamed at Herb, "You trusted me with the job! Now let me do it!" I had received a lovely gift, and to have it snatched away was more than I could bear.

Herb looked stunned. He turned and slowly walked away.

I was stunned, too, and shocked at myself. I hadn't been moved by such violent anger since one day twenty years before when Grandma Dimock tried to order me around, and I pushed her bodily into the bedroom and slammed the door.

No longer having any enthusiasm for the task at hand, I stumbled over to the army-surplus hammock we had suspended between two trees, and lay down to let my passion subside. As I rocked gently, my mind went over the scene we had just come through. Part of me asked, "How could I have behaved so harshly to Herb, the person I love most in all the world?" But another part of me insisted, "He was wrong to act like a drill sergeant! I'm glad I flared up!"

I thought of the many occasions during his ministry when I had dropped everything to come at his call and listen to his outline or progress on a sermon. I remembered feeling resentment at being pulled away from my own projects, but I had stifled it. At the time, I thought I was being "unselfish," and helpful toward the goals we both believed in. Now I was beginning to see that I had not been true to my own integrity. Had I actually encouraged Herb to treat me like a flunky, a slave? My exposure to the growing Women's Liberation movement had planted seeds that were at last beginning to germinate.

Later that afternoon, as we sat side by side on a big rock under our oak trees, we shared perspectives on our clash.

"This has been a big eye opener for me," Herb said gently. "I've just realized how often I dominate you. I give orders and expect you to obey."

I was relieved at his confession, and reached out to grasp his hand. "I know. And I have usually yielded, because I—" How could I tell him? "Because I tend to put you on a pedestal. As if you are an authority who has all the answers. As if you are a saint who can do no wrong."

"Ho-ho! You know that's not true!" He put an arm around my shoulder and pulled me close. "I'm glad you showed your tiger. It's jolted me into seeing what bad habits I've gotten into." He looked into my eyes earnestly, and said with anguish in his voice, "I don't want to dominate you any more at all."

With a common resolution to reform, we celebrated our sweet reconciliation with hugs and kisses, and were at peace.

But that startling incident was only a hint of the turmoil that would entangle us during the years after we took up permanent residence at Anathoth.

We moved into our unfinished but habitable house on September 14, 1976. The excitement of selling the Belvidere Avenue house, resigning from our jobs, and transporting all our worldly goods to Anathoth, which had absorbed us for months, had now diminished. The men who worked with us on the construction had been dismissed. Gone was the racket of saws and hammers, clattering boards, and noisy engines of delivery trucks and bulldozers.

That first night, as we lay down in our own new bedroom, I gazed at the quiet stars through the narrow but numerous windows, and rejoiced that we could now start living the ideal life I had envisioned.

Within two days, however, Herb and I were snapping at each other. When we tried to move a table through a doorway, Herb directed, "Over this way!"

I thought he meant that I should move in the direction he nodded, so I did. But it didn't help.

"I said this way!" he barked.

"Oh. Move the table that way?"

"Of course!" He was getting impatient at my denseness.

I replied with equal impatience. "Well, how was I to know?"

Later, as we unpacked books and placed them on the sturdy shelves we had inherited from Fairy Godmother Jones, I rushed in to say, "That shelf is dusty. Let me run this rag over it first."

"It'll only get dusty again," Herb threw back. "Why stop to do that now?"

I pressed with the logic that seemed obvious to me. "Because," I fussed, "we'll get it all over our fingers, and leave dirty marks on everything we touch."

He cut me down with a withering glance.

After several of such incidents, we both knew we were out of line. I finally said, "Herb, I think we're both tired from all the work on building over the past three months. We're foolish to keep pushing at the same speed just because we see so many unfinished things to do. Can't we stop for a meditation period now and then?"

"You're absolutely right, Maggie!" he said contritely. "We need to slow down our pace and 'shore up our institutions.'" After a minute or two of reflection, he suggested, " How about setting aside twenty minutes, twice a day, to sit quietly and renew our spirits?"

Our establishment of "Matins" at 9:00 a.m. and "Vespers" at 5:00 p.m. really helped. Perhaps we were going to have our "hermitage," after all.

Then one day Herb looked up from our account book, and said in a horrified tone, "We're almost out of money!"

I was not surprised. I knew that our savings had been completely used up; in fact, we had already borrowed $3000 from Herb's brother Donald, to meet the most recent construction expenses. The processing of Herb's application for Social Security would take several months. For now, our only income was my modest Washington State pension. Still, I wasn't worried. I knew how to postpone purchases and stretch money. "Be not anxious about what you will eat..."

But Herb was definitely anxious. In his customary thinking of himself as "head" of the family, he just had to do something to bring in immediate cash. After making several phone calls, he shouted to me in the next room, triumphantly, "I've got a job!" It was not until that moment, when I heard the great relief in his voice, that I realized how near panic he had been.

The job was to run the back-hoe for Ernie, next-door neighbor of Lois and Harry. Leaning on his experience with a back-hoe on our own land, Herb confidently undertook that labor for several hours a day.

I could see that it was tiring him. "Maybe it's too much for you," I suggested one evening at suppertime.

He tried to deny that possibility. "I'll be O.K. when I get used to it." I took his assurance as valid and did not protest.

When that job came to an end in a week and a half, Herb found employment painting a house, then doing carpentry hours on end. By the time a flexing saw blade gave him a cut finger and a bruised eye, he had to admit such strenuous activity *was* too much for him, and he gave it up.

Becoming a school-bus driver was his next occupation, one that I thought sounded easier, as well as "romantic." I did not realize the inconvenience of the split shifts, nor the hazards of manipulating the large bus on narrow, winding roads—especially with a crowd of noisy, active, unpredictable children to cope with at the same time. Herb showed the strain, and I was glad when he quit after three months.

Ironically, a wonderful benefit for me resulted from Herb's being away from home at those stressful jobs. I finished writing the final three chapters of "Large Love from Laura Jane"! I felt as though I had given birth. The "baby"— after four years' gestation—emerged healthy and attractive. I made arrangements to have sixty copies of the 150-page manuscript printed, with photographs, and distributed them to friends and relatives, charging $5.00 to those who could afford it. Even Herb was pleased with my production. I was exultant.

The coming of April 1977 was full of promise. The beginning of Herb's monthly Social Security checks, as well as a retroactive payment for nearly a year's unpaid eligibility, relieved our financial situation. And the sweet sunshine of spring beckoned us to begin our garden. I helped Herb put a fence around the area we had selected, and we ordered seeds from the Burpee catalog. In May we devoted ourselves to the lengthy task of removing rocks and weeds, and then, with stakes and string, marked the rows where we would plant carrots, turnips, lettuce, chard and a dozen other vegetables. I was delighted that my dream of "raising our own vegetables" was about to become true.

My original thought was that we would spend four hours a day on gardening, and have an additional four hours available for writing. I was drinking in so thoroughly the joys of "living in the country," I wanted to write it all down in a book to be called "Anathoth Sketches." But I hadn't counted on how demanding the garden was going to be. We had to lug hoses around for watering. We had to make the wire fence deer-proof. Then came the battles with grasshoppers and gophers, weeding, more weeding, harvesting, and processing. Only four hours a day? Ha!

Yet I could hardly pull back, once we'd got started. I did enjoy being close to the soil and watching the miracle of growth. I relished the taste of our wonderful corn and tomatoes and green beans. I was glad our enterprise had been a "success." But I often felt like a slave to it, and was disappointed that I had little time to write.

Herb, on the other hand, was so proud of our first year's production, he decided to enlarge the garden the second year. He pictured to me in glowing terms the thrill it would be to add loganberries, celery, eggplant, artichokes, and asparagus, and I was sucked into consenting.

Our original slogan of "two can do it" took the form of an assumption that we should both do everything together. I didn't realize how much Herb was setting the agenda and dragging me along.

Yet in the background I felt the continual nagging and nudging of the question, "Where can I find time to write my 'Sketches,' and more family biographies?" It did not occur to either of us that the activities I personally was drawn to had as much validity as Herb's. And I was used to being patient. "Love is very patient, very kind," the apostle Paul had written. I didn't see that it might be an error to be too patient.

But it wasn't the garden alone that kept us both as busy as we had ever been before retirement. The appeal of constructive community activities was irresistible. Herb became chairman of the "G-Plan Barter Group," and then secretary-treasurer of the Board of a newly-formed cooperative market, the "Briar Patch." He became clerk of the Grass Valley Friends Meeting soon after we had joined that Quaker group. His responsibilities in these organizations inevitably drew me in for secretarial assistance. How could I refuse? It was more than just my custom of "helping Herb" with whatever he was doing. I believed in these organizations too!

I felt as though I was on a merry-go-round that was colorful and fascinating. Yet something was missing, and the merry-go-round wouldn't stop long enough for me to see what it was.

Because I always believed events and situations were sent into our lives for a purpose, my continual informal cry to God was, "What is it you want to teach me?"

Our daughter Marti provided one part of the answer to my prayer. Visiting us at Anathoth, she and Herb and I sat talking in our living room. Herb carried on most of the conversation with her. I wanted to put in my two-cents' worth, and opened my mouth to begin, but Herb brushed me off with a gesture and kept going. Marti wouldn't let him get away with that. "No, let her speak!" she commanded her dad. And he let me have my say.

It was a wonderful feeling to have someone come to my rescue, to take my part, to be my advocate! Later, when I was bidding Marti goodbye, she gave me a hug and said slyly, "It takes two to make a doormat, you know, Mom."

She shocked me awake. Had I been a doormat? Had I let Herb walk all over me?

As I lay in bed in the middle of that night, I recalled scene after scene in which he had actually tromped on me. There was the day he was concentrating on something at his desk, and I inadvertently rustled some papers. When he scowled and snapped his fingers at me as if I'd done it on purpose, I felt belittled. Another time he told me to move a potted plant off the table, and when I was puzzled and asked why, he hollered, "Just do as I say!" Often he tried to control my actions: "In that telephone call to Lois, you talked too long!" Any protest I had made in those situations was mild, weak. Yes, I had been a doormat. I saw I was partly responsible for our clashes, and determined to find a better way.

An opportunity that I almost didn't recognize came when Herb and I made a vacation trip to Oregon and Washington to visit children and grandchildren. Our contacts with these dear ones were enjoyable and heartwarming. But as we drove back into California and I took my turn at the wheel, a major explosion occurred. Herb, who had been a perfect angel the whole trip, even telling me I was a good driver, suddenly turned into a dictator. He criticized my cautious driving, and my following the letter of the law.

"It wasn't necessary to stop at that stop sign," he scolded me. "You'd already stopped ten feet before, to talk to the agricultural officer."

I argued back hotly, "I've trained myself to stop automatically at stop signs. That way I don't have to think about it every time."

"That's ridiculous," he countered.

I kept up a whining defense. "It seemed logical to stop and look around, in case another car or person was going to dart forth."

A little farther on, we met a flagman, who was holding his sign in an ambiguous manner. I couldn't tell whether he intended "slow," or was in process of turning it to "stop." So I stopped the car until I could be sure. "Go ahead—don't stop!" Herb shouted.

I could stand it no longer. Tears rained down my face as we passed the construction area, and finally I burst out, "I feel as if you're saying I'm no good because I don't see it your way!'"

At last Herb realized how tyrannical and oppressive he had been. "I'm sorry I've been jabbing at you," he said penitently. "I was impatient with you because I wanted to get home faster, to check up on the garden we left in the hands of our housesitters." He patted my shoulder gently. "I was completely out of order."

I was not pleased with the tearful way I had asserted myself, but at least I had gotten through to Herb. We forgave each other, and peace reigned again.

One night when Herb couldn't sleep, I was more aware than usual of the call for the doormat to strike back, and did so deliberately. Often my scratching his back helped him relax and settle down. It got so that he'd simply turn on his side, offering me his back, and order, "Scratch!" Sometimes I was tired and would rather not, but I was habitually moved by the Christian principle of "self-sacrifice" to cancel out what I saw as my "ego" desires, and give him what he seemed to need.

But this particular night I screwed up my courage and rebelled. "I don't want to!" I announced strongly. How would he take it? Would he give me the cold silent treatment?

He reacted with curiosity. "What's the matter?"

I poured my feelings out in a flood. "Herb, you just assume I'm always available to rub your back or scratch it, as if I'm your—your valet! Don't you ever realize that I might be tired myself and not feel like doing it? You're taking my service for granted! You're treating me like an obedient dog who's ordered to 'Sit' and he sits. You order 'Scratch' and I scratch. Tonight I don't feel like it, and you'll have to get along without it."

I was aghast at my own uncharacteristic "selfishness." Yet there was something good and right about it, too.

Herb seemed surprised, as if he'd never seen his demands on me in that light. When my stream of protest had run its course, he said sweetly, "You've always been such a helper and healer to me, honey. I see that I have taken you for granted, and I don't want to do that. How do you suggest I change my way of letting you knew when I have a need?"

We discussed it lovingly, and agreed on an acceptable alternative. In the future he would ask, "Do you feel like scratching my back?" and I would choose to say yes or no, and he would accept my answer with understanding.

"I might even ask if you'd like a similar service from me," he volunteered.

We were in harmony again, and the new way worked beautifully from that time on. I knew there would be other areas and other issues in which I still needed to affirm myself. But I had made a start in reclaiming my own soul.

Herb made a real start, too. Toward our fortieth wedding anniversary, his progress was highlighted one Saturday morning when I was combing the tangles out of my long hair in front of our bedroom mirror. I had started letting it grow ten years earlier, because Herb was always saying, "I like women to have long hair." As time went on, I found it difficult to handle. My hair was too fine. But I felt compelled to yield to his preference. Imagine my surprise and relief when, on that Saturday morning, he watched me thoughtfully and then declared, "You know, I think I've been dominating you about your hair. Why don't you go ahead and do whatever you want with it?"

I had it cut. And he even liked it that way! Now I saw how foolish I was to let his opinion control me for so long. I had new hope that we were both ready for further growth.

And I got started on writing "Anathoth Sketches."

Walls Tumble Down
(1979-88)

By the time of our fortieth anniversary Margaret had found half the answer of what had skewed our marriage. I struggled well into the next decade to discover the other half. It was my turn to "grow up." With my left brain I had blamed the culture for my patriarchal ways. Now I had to accept responsibility in my heart or our union would wither.

Who was it who said, "Stone walls do not a prison make"? But in my case my stone walls of habit had imprisoned me. The terrible thing about habit is that it starts out soft as a spring cloud but ends up hard as stone. Breaking down stony walls of habit was my task, and I was given a first assignment in October of 1979.

We returned home from a vacation trip to Southern California to visit Margaret's eighty-nine year old father and his new wife. We walked into our parlor and into the surprise of our lives. Marti and Zoe and family and friends had conspired to raise a fund to celebrate the anniversary. On a card table decorated with balloons and colorful crepe paper streamers was a check for $3400 and a letter of instructions.

"Out of the country?" I cried as Margaret and I collapsed onto the sofa. The letter was explicit. The purse was to be used only for recreational travel abroad. This cut sharply across our lifetime habit of not spending money on ourselves. Our children were wiser than we knew.

"That's what it says," my beloved confirmed, waving the paper in my face. "Out of the USA."

"Wow! I never dreamed this could happen. Travel!"

"But where?"

"Yeah. Like the Caribbean?" I ventured in a burst of recklessness.

"Or England?" said Margaret, picking up on the dream. "I'd love to browse around in the country of my ancestors." Her voice was full of eager enthusiasm.

For the moment that was it. Two very different images to be satisfied. So, as we brought our luggage in from the Plymouth, we let the whole idea rest for a while and busied ourselves with supper prep.

While we sat at table, working at our plates of pinto beans and baked potato, I stared across the room to our towering bookcase where a twelve volume set of the Interpreter's Bible whispered back to me about my lifelong training and career, and a new idea was born out of my old habits.

"Why not," I proposed, "instead of England, why not go to the land of our *spiritual* ancestors—yours and mine?"

A peculiar smile spread over Margaret's face. "Israel?"

That was the beginning of my first stonewall encounter. Once again I was setting the agenda, and my mate was probably saying to herself, "If my husband wants to do thus-and-so of course I will support him." I was pushing, she was yielding.

On Margaret's birthday, March 24, 1980, we flew to New York and boarded one of the giant 747s for Tel Aviv. The plane was full of Jewish pilgrims on the way to the Holy Land to celebrate the Passover, men with yarmulkes perched on their heads, women in dark dresses and dark hats. Already we were being prepared for our adventure. Two days later, comfortably established in a bed-and-breakfast home in Jerusalem, we were ready to begin a hands-on exploration of the ancient city.

Walls were everywhere. The old city, constricted behind huge, stony ramparts, was separated from a sprawling modern Jerusalem. Invisible walls of fear isolated Arabs and Jews from each other. And deep traditions rooted in separate histories kept hatreds very much alive. But I was oblivious to my own walls.

I became an authoritative tour guide, steering our adventure from step to step, deciding for us to visit the Dome of the Rock, the old City of David outside the present walls, and the Pool of Siloam, and the Garden of Gethsemane. The program became costly. By mid-week Margaret fell sick with an intestinal disorder which sent her to bed and out of my reach. She turned me loose to roam and, with the help of new friends, I jaunted north to visit the Quaker Meeting in Ramallah and then back in time to get caught up in a Palm Sunday celebration of pilgrims reenacting Jesus' entrance into Jerusalem.

I was haunted by a deep unease that somehow my attitudes had contributed to Margaret's illness. I began asking questions of myself.

Nevertheless, when she recovered we rented a tiny Fiat and roamed from Dan to Beersheba. With growing enthusiasm I led the way to the heights of Masada, where the last Jewish stronghold of the first century A.D. was finally conquered by the Roman legions. We swam in the Dead Sea, or rather, floated on top of the salty water. I took us around the Sea of Galilee, and then probed into the Golan Heights where we got lost in a dense fog until a jeep load of Israeli soldiers showed us the way out.

Our visit to the locale of the Sermon on the Mount near Capernaum brought our trip, for me, to an unforgettable climax. As we stood knee-deep in spring grasses, near an orchard of grapefruit that spread down the hillside, we could look south to the far end of the Sea of Galilee. It was the morning of Good Friday, and as I began to review what happened to Jesus that day I was horrified by the thought that my domination of Margaret was a kind of crucifixion. It was too painful to talk about. I reached for her hand and held tight as I prayed for forgiveness and guidance.

Near the finale of our three weeks we took a special little trip to visit the original Anathoth after which we had named our home. Now in the twentieth century it was only a modest mound of shattered walls, buried ruins waiting for some archeologist to dig in. Would the erosion of time do the same for my walls?

Soon after our return my divine Guide laid out another challenge to my imprisoning habits. I plunged into aggressive work to organize the Domestic Violence Coalition to serve the Grass Valley-Nevada City community. I was eager to come to the defense of battered women, and, in total blindness, dragged my "battered woman" along. We became "house parents" in the Safe House program as a stream of women and their children were referred to us for shelter. The burden fell heavily on Margaret. I was robbing her of valuable time she needed to devote to her writing.

I did not see the irony of what I was doing, but Margaret did and began a frontal attack on my walls. As chairman of the DVC Board I got in over my head. We needed to find money for office rent and salary for the Executive Director. My first plan for a fund raiser was to raffle off a house in Grass Valley; sell tickets to cover the cost of purchase and use the excess for DVC expenses.

I don't know who originated the idea, but when I came home, full of my customary drive, and laid out the picture for Margaret's comments, her response floored me.

"Herb, that's madness! Who is going to sell the chances? Who is going to buy them? The amount of work will be gigantic. This is a prescription for disaster. *Your* disaster! It will be my disaster too! Do you expect me to pick up the pieces of *you* when it's all over? I will not be your doormat!"

The next day I scratched the raffle idea. Other programs followed, leading me characteristically into deeper exhaustion, until Margaret rebelled.

"Herb," she chided severely, "you've got to get out. This enterprise is killing you! And it's driving me crazy."

"Yeah. You know it." The truth is I had a neck problem with a thinned disk. The pain was constant.

Margaret was not silent. "Let somebody else be chairman. Quit playing God, as though only you can do it."

She replanted in my consciousness the realization that I was still the addictive workaholic. I quit the DVC. I had to. My body had added its protest to

Margaret's. But of course, as one might predict, I didn't give up my drive to work. After my neck felt better I found other projects.

Surely I can do better. Can't I? The answer came—but slowly. The inner voice in my soul was speaking more frequently and with persistence.

First was the unfinished business I still had with Mother. She had been gone for more than twelve years, but the deep warfare we had carried on, beginning with the year of my marriage to Margaret, and up to two years before her death, still weighed heavily in my soul.

And then one day the unsought-for answer embraced me. I was deep into gardening. I called out to Margaret where she worked at her station at the kitchen sink, "I'm going to pull weeds!" Through the window she waved me on my way. I crossed our patio lawn and started down the sloping path at the east end of the house.

In the middle of that trek the divine Hand stopped me in my tracks, as though to say, "Listen!" What I heard was awesome. The words were clear and bold, that I had forgiven Mother and she had forgiven me for all of our past harshnesses. One stony barrier was gone. My joy was full and overflowing. The important pulling of weeds had happened in my soul, not in the soil of the garden. I returned to the kitchen and shared the good news with Margaret.

That experience of forgiveness with Mother, I am sure, made me ready for the final attack on my walls of habit, which began in January of '84 when I went to see Doctor Banister for my annual check up. I told him I had no major complaint, only that I had a dogged feeling within me that I was not doing very well with life. He was an excellent counselor and heard me out patiently as I detailed my petty pains: recurring sinus distress, tension in my neck from the thinned out disk, cold feet.

His response was classic and full of humor. "Sounds as though we need to have a going-away-party for your ego. Margaret would welcome that, wouldn't she?"

We both laughed, in fact we laughed almost to the verge of hysteria. He had hit me dead center, and I felt a happy relief. But as he pursued his medical examination he used a new tool called the "hemoccult test." To his and my surprise he discovered blood in my stool. His counsel was that we should plan to wait a month and do a second test. In the middle of February I returned and the result was "no more blood." He told me the earlier test could have been a fluke, and that I didn't need to worry.

I didn't worry. I put it out of my mind for more than a year. And then, without any symptoms of any kind to nudge me, I spoke to Margaret one day.

"I hear that the hemoccult test kit is available at the pharmacy. I think I'll get one and test myself."

Margaret the skeptic was present in force. "Oh? What do you want to do that for?"

"I don't know. It's just a hunch."

She shrugged. "At least it can't do any harm."

I brought the kit home and found that it had three test units. I did my own examination three days in a row. Each one turned out bloody-positive. My doctor referred me to a specialist who promptly took me to the Sierra Memorial Hospital and did a colonoscopy. The bad news. Colon cancer. Well developed.

I carried the news back to Margaret and found her concentrating on a book of sonnets she was writing. I unloaded my deep puzzlement. "But why me? We always ate the right foods, never smoked or drank or did any of the things that...."

She left her desk, came close to where I stood in dark pondering, and put her arms around me. She had no answer for my question, but she gave the big answer for my spirit.

A week later, while Margaret paced the hospital hallway with daughter Marti, a surgeon removed almost half of my large intestine. He reported that the growth had very nearly penetrated the colon wall and might then have metastacized. He hoped we had caught it soon enough. The speed of this whole experience was amazing.

The next day when Margaret came to the side of my hospital bed, both of us were profoundly shaken. She was exhausted with the grinding uncertainty, and I was in pain. For the first time in my life the reality of mortality closed in around me. With tubes stuck in the veins of my arm and a six inch incision across my abdomen, I knew that the grim reaper had come into my neighborhood.

I complained to my helpmate as she stroked my forehead. "I feel awful."

Margaret was a better doctor than the pros. She knew that what I needed was a transfusion of the spirit, something to put my mind on. She proposed that we sing one of our favorite hymns. Flat on my back, I pulled myself together and we began.

> Galilee, bright Galilee,
> Hallowed thoughts we turn to thee,
> Woven through thy history,
> Gleams the charming mystery
> Of the life of one who came,
> Bearing grief, reproach and shame....
>
> Still his touch upon the soul
> Bringeth balm and maketh whole.
> Still he comforts mourning hearts,
> Life and joy and peace imparts....

Both of us broke down into uncontrolled weeping. The darkest hour of our lives, we now began to believe, was in the hands of our Creator, and I was assured that healing would come. This encounter was for some bigger purpose, and we would work together to find the message.

During the nine days that followed in my hospital recovery, I had plenty of time to meditate and plenty of time to read. Somehow there came into my hands a treatise about colon cancer, and in the midst of it there was a shocking statement. It jumped out of the page and hit me smack in the face. "Type A personalities are highly susceptible to this form of cancer."

That was when the light finally dawned. My workaholism, my drive for achievement, was the very essence of the "Type A" kind of person. I had invited the disease into my body by my lifelong addiction to work. The news ripped an unclosable hole in my habitual consciousness.

I saw in vivid outline the connection. My drive for achievement and my domination of my mate were one and the same thing. To win in this world, I had told myself, one has to be in control of all parts of the action. That is the essence of patriarchy. Rule the roost!

Now I felt the doormat and the dominator in our family at last would be able to join hands and build a new life.

My recovery was a long drawn-out affair. Regularly I checked back with the surgeon, weekly, then monthly, and finally, quarterly. He tested my blood for the return of telltale cancer antigens. For a long while the readings hovered in the totally safe range. With that news, predictably, I let my guards down and allowed old patterns of work to return. We had ended our vegetable garden so that I could devote myself to work at writing: drama, novel, short story, but unwisely I did it with the same intensity of my old activist self.

And then there came a day, on my regular visit to the doctor, when the report on my antigen reading was 6.1, barely within the safe range. But, he said, "We should watch this carefully." On my next visit the figure had jumped to 8.5. That's when he became really concerned. "Looks like a possible recurrence," he said. "We should take steps right away."

In my heart I knew what was the matter, and I said to him, "Let's wait one more month."

I went home to Margaret. "I need your help," I said. "You know how it is with alcoholics. I'm a recovering workaholic, and I fell off the wagon."

She captured my restless hands in her grip and responded with the special power she always brought into our marriage dialogue: logic. "I've been watching your driving passion for the past couple of months. What can you do that's the exact opposite?"

"Do? That's the problem. I'm always doing!"

"What if you take a day to do nothing?"

"Do nothing, for a whole day?" That was totally against my style.

"Sure. And then another and another."

In her wisdom Margaret had led me into a new pattern. We invented the DND—the Do-Nothing-Day. It was the hardest work I ever undertook. For that critical month I lived the life of the recovering workaholic. Completely. Totally. I took a folding chair over into the woods, far away from the telephone and my desk. I read a couple of novels. I dug out an inflatable plastic raft and went floating on our pond.

When I returned to the doctor he was unbelieving. My antigen reading had dropped from 8.5 to 3.6. I had done my inner work very well. That was when my big breakthrough became inwardly real. I had proven irrefutably that my drivenness was the source of my problem with my health and my wife.

The payoff was magnificent. Margaret and I were in love as never before, deeper than in our days of courtship, higher than our most extravagant imagining. As we sat together in our glistening white patio chairs, sipping from tumblers of cranapple juice, I looked at her with new eyes.

"You know," I ventured, "for almost fifty years I have followed the illusion that I know who you are."

"What are you driving at?" Her eyes were radiant.

"I mean, I behaved as though I could predict how you would feel and act in any situation. I was wrong. You are a stranger. A unique person every day."

"I love it!"

"Now I see you as my beloved stranger."

Margaret took us the next step. "And isn't that the way it should be in all our relationships? We should never pigeonhole anyone."

In the days that followed an equally profound change emerged in the progress of my writing. I had not understood why always something had gotten in the way to keep me from my playwright's dream. Now I saw that my drive-and-domination was precisely what my writer's block was all about.

I picked up storytelling again in a relaxed, open frame of mind. I completed a fantasy novel and screenplay, titled "Seven Days In June," about how a group of teenagers marched around the Pentagon until the "walls came tumbling down."

After that I poured my deepest devotion into a stage play, "The Two Fools." It told the story of a clown in first century Jerusalem whose friendship with Lazarus put him on the trail of Jesus until at last he found him, and shared one of the three crosses on Calvary.

I reveled in the return of my dream that I had laid aside when I found my mate and my career in the ministry in 1939. I was so profoundly convinced that Fools was a good drama that I helped to establish a new theater group, the Gateway Players, devoted to producing original drama.

I found lots of willing thespians who would grab at any chance to get on stage. In the spring of '87 we presented our drama to the community, with a cast of twenty on the stage of the Miners Foundry Cultural Center. The local Grass Valley newspaper ran a special feature about the Dimock couple with our picture, for not only did I have a stage play to offer but Margaret in this same period had found a publisher for her book of sonnets, "Lord, Behold Our Family," based on a prayer by Robert Louis Stevenson.

A series of six audiences at the Miners Foundry gave modest applause for "The Two Fools". Our first production was passable. One year later I rewrote the finale into a dream scene in which the Fool and Jesus come down from their respective crosses to get intimately acquainted. The Fool teaches Jesus how to juggle. Jesus teaches the Fool the meaning of love and life. We had a winner.

The result of this second production was rousing acclaim from our audiences and three nominations by the Sacramento Area Regional Theater Alliance (SARTA). We were considered for best original script, best original production and best lead actor. For me my playwright's passion had come to full fruitage—after fifty years. And even more lasting I had found a friend, a male friend, Gil, whom I could count on day after day to keep me grounded, for he also was a writer and a lover of the theater.

Golden Marriage and Beyond (1989)

As Herb and I launched into the year 1989, our fiftieth wedding anniversary loomed on the horizon with a special challenge.

Our theater friend, Gil, showed up at our back door one day, and with his customary enthusiasm volunteered to organize a gala celebration for us in Grass Valley on October 15. He would rent a hall.

I was taken aback. Hesitantly I addressed Gil, not wanting to reject his generous proposal. "Well," I fumbled, "we've already accepted our daughter Zoe's offer to have a celebration at her place in Oregon."

Herb saw no problem. "That one's to be in August," he explained to Gil, "mostly a sort of family reunion." His glance included me as he went on, "It would be quite suitable to have another event in October, for theater people and a big bunch of friends, as well as local relatives."

To me that sounded like a lot of work. But my mind was relieved when Gil told us, "I'll take care of all the arrangements. You don't have to do a thing."

For a time I really believed that. No responsibilities. What a pleasant prospect!

A week or two later, however, Gil telephoned to ask, "Can you work up a list of the people you'd like us to send invitations to? With their addresses?" And a few days after that, "Your sister Lois has agreed to lead group singing. Would you make a list of some of your favorite songs?"

Ah, well, that wouldn't be too hard, I thought. And when he suggested we gather some photos and slides of our family life in earlier years, I saw that as a fun project.

Then came the big one. Gil got up from our dining table after an evening's critiquing of a play Herb was writing, and said as he made ready to depart, "Oh, there's just one thing I'd like to have you do. Will you prepare a fifteen-minute skit or dialogue for the two of you to present as part of the program on October 15?"

Whoa! So we would not escape responsibility!

"What did you have in mind?" Herb asked carefully.

"Something that would let people know *how you did it*. Young folks these days ask questions like, 'How did you stand it for fifty years?' So, you tell them!"

After Gil had left, Herb and I looked at each other in amazement. "I never thought of marriage as a thing to be stood, or endured," I said.

"Neither did I." Herb shook his head. "So Gil thinks we can convey all we've learned from fifty years of living together in *fifteen minutes*?"

I laughed. "Impossible! But I suppose we have to try."

Many weeks lay ahead before Gil's assignment was due, so I tucked it into the back of my mind and went on with my current living. My father had died the previous year, at the age of ninety-eight, and I was now focused on writing the story of his life.

Yet I found myself grappling with the subject Gil had raised, willy-nilly. It had a way of emerging unexpectedly in the most ordinary circumstances.

Early one morning, I opened my eyes to find Herb already awake and gazing at me. I poked him in the ribs and exclaimed in mock surprise, "I'm in bed with a seventy-five-year-old man!"

His affectionate response was, "Did I remember to tell you that I love you?"

We were lying in my grandparents' carved antique bed, now altered to accomodate a queen-size mattress. Many of our most meaningful moments had taken place in that bed. Sex, of course—and we were delighted that, in recent years, long-baffling snags had given way, and we were more often blessed with the magic of our "second night" in Honeymoon Cottage.

But there were other kinds of intimacy too. We sang hymns together at times when we both couldn't sleep. On some nights Herb complained of "peas under the mattress" that were making him uncomfortable, and I laid my hand on his neck or shoulder or back to calm him. At dawn we frequently reported beautiful, or distressing, dreams, or shared practical ideas, such as how to hire more regular help with the outdoor work or the housecleaning.

This particular morning our conversation drifted to mutual admiration.

"You look cute with you night cap on crooked," I told him.

"I like your profile," he said, tracing its outline with his finger.

"Your blue pajamas accent the blue of your eyes," I pursued.

He smiled. "I'm glad you're here."

That simple statement set loose a flood of associations in my mind. Our advancing age had made us both keenly aware that, at some future time, one of us might not be "here" with the other. I was constantly grateful to have such a precious companion, not only in bed, but throughout our days of work and play, and in little humorous references to innumerable joint experiences of the past.

"I'm glad I married you!" I said, cuddling up close.

Herb put his arms around me, and our kisses were both vigorous and tender.

Lying back on his pillow, Herb asked, "Why do you suppose we're so happily married?"

I thought a minute, as I let my eyes wander to the weird shadows cast on the ceiling by the rising sun. "Maybe it's because each of us was committed to growing spiritually even before we met."

My dear one nodded, and added another piece of the puzzle. "And then Fritz Kunkel gave us tools for recognizing our egos and shifting to a level beyond them."

"And besides that," I said, "we always had the common goal of wanting to help all humanity evolve toward cosmic consciousness."

"We still do," Herb said softly. "We still do." He stretched his limbs as he asked, "Is there any way we can get all that into the dialogue Gil wants us to do?"

I rolled my eyes. "I don't know. It covers so much. We'll have to let it marinate awhile." But I thought we had stumbled onto at least some of what the people needed to hear.

Two weeks later our halos slipped. Herb fell into a pattern of drivenness that left him exhausted by nightfall. He collapsed into bed and slept for a few hours, but by the middle of the night we were both awake and restless. Herb poured out a confession of his "sins": He had crowded too many errands into his morning trip to town, and then spent the afternoon pushing to build a new shelf under the computer desk, and before supper he sat down to tackle financial records. No wonder he cut a deep gash in his finger while slicing carrots for dinner!

Now, in our unlighted bedroom, he cried out in unbelief, "How could I have tried to do so much today? It's the parish-ministry syndrome! I think I have to make things happen, so as to save the world!"

"I know what you mean," I sympathized. Stroking his brow, I recalled my own type of being driven: trying to accomplish all the little chores and errands, telephone calls, and correspondence that I felt I "ought" to do.

"And here comes this skit we're supposed to create for our anniversary. Ha!" he snorted. "Who are we to tell other people how to live?"

"Yeah." I shifted my body to face him more directly in the dark. "It makes you wonder whether we've learned anything at all."

"We fall short so often!" Herb sighed. He sounded depressed. "Does anybody ever 'get there'?"

I was silent, thinking of how many times Herb and I, for all our lofty ideals, continued to misunderstand each other or to get irritated over some small thing.

All at once some angel of grace wafted an encouraging thought into my mind, and I shared it with my partner. "Remember the prayer a preacher made that sounded like losing one's underwear? 'Lord, forgive us for our falling shorts'?"

Herb chuckled. "Yes. And we have been forgiven, over and over again. We've learned to forgive each other, too."

"So maybe we have improved some," I declared hopefully. "Whether we ever reach the ultimate goal or not, the striving itself is worthwhile. The reach is what makes life rich."

I could feel Herb relaxing. Quietly he added his bit to my upbeat conclusion. "The fact that we strive together, and help each other up when we stumble—that's what keeps our marriage growing and flourishing!"

"Two can do it," I murmured, and we settled into sleep.

In the days that followed, we made fresh efforts not to "run ahead of the grace of God," a phrase Herb's mentor, Charles Whiston, liked to use. One Saturday, we had enough sense to leave unfinished our task of cleaning up the garage. Two hours was long enough! We strolled across the patio lawn to our braided-rope hammock, lay down on it, side by side, and set it swinging as we rested.

I looked up at the sunlight on the leaves of the oaks and "trees of heaven" overhead, with the blue of the sky showing through the branches. "How I love our land!" I thought. Being close to trees and rocks and fields had brought me much joy during the thirteen years we'd lived at Anathoth. Sometimes I'd been slow to pick up on Herb's enthusiastic innovations, like buying the two wooded acres adjacent to our original purchase, and having a pond excavated. But usually such enterprises had turned out to be cherished blessings. I treasured walking through the woods. I adored swimming in our pond.

Herb interrupted my reverie. "A penny for your thoughts."

I flashed him a smile, and said, "I was thinking how much I love our land, and our trees, and our pond." Oh, I might as well tell him the rest. "And I've been remembering what different personalities we have. You barge ahead and rush into things impulsively, where I'm cautious and think things over first."

Herb ran his fingers through my hair. "We sure have different styles, haven't we? It's been a problem when we each think our own style is better than the other's. But I think we're coming to respect each other's style."

"Yes, respect it," I agreed, "and listen to it, and then take appropriate action. We don't have to adopt the other person's style, nor insist the other adopt ours."

Herb came out with a vivid metaphor. "I read an article about wolves. The pack needs one bold wolf to go in front and lead the way, and one timid one to stay in the rear and warn against too much daring. That's us!"

I was pleased to see that he was no longer criticizing my lagging behind, but was praising and accepting my function.

"We're each unique, aren't we?" I said with new awe. I wondered if we could find a way to put something of this in our October skit.

But first would come our reunion at Zoe's in Oregon. Herb had approved of my plan for posters, which could be used in October too, displaying photographs from our early, middle, and recent years. In July he obtained the cardboard and helped me select the pictures.

"Look at these snapshots taken in Antioch," I said as we spread them out on the dining table. "Don't our children look happy and smiling? And you too, here where you're washing our car the Arlington folks gave us. Even me, sweeping the porch."

Herb put his arm around my shoulder. "Everybody smiles for picture-taking," he said wryly. "These don't show the struggles we had in Antioch."

I remembered how tired I felt all the time, and the daily strain of supervising the kids unendingly.

"And yet the pictures are not really false," I insisted. "There was a lot of laughter and fun and love there, in spite of anything."

Herb seemed reluctant to agree, but finally he said, "Yes, that's true too. As we were saying the other day, life is mixed."

Our posters went with us to Oregon, and did their part in creating a festive atmosphere. I felt blessed as I watched a dozen of our grandchildren and grand-nieces/nephews flit from one game or project to another, while their parents caught up on long-missed conversation. Zoe and her family were gracious hosts, guiding all thirty-five of us through wonderful activities and rituals. An aura of warmth surrounded the whole weekend.

As we drove home to California, I said to Herb, "I'm glad we had this gathering at Zoe's. She doesn't have as much contact with the whole clan as some of the rest do."

Herb confirmed my feeling. "Very important," he said. "It was a lot of work for her, but I'm sure she knows, now, that she really is part of our extended family."

Before we knew it, we were turning our calendar pages in September. One afternoon Herb arrived home from a lunch date in town with Gil.

"Gil says they're estimating about a hundred people will attend our October 15 anniversary," he announced. "Margaret, we've got to get busy and work up our dialogue!"

I knew that was true, but I felt baffled. "How do you think we should go about it? What's the first step?"

Herb was quickly ready with a suggestion. "Why don't we each write a sample dialogue, and then see which is better. Or maybe combine the best ideas of both."

I tried. As many mornings as possible, I went out to the ten-by-twelve-foot "studio" Herb had fixed up for me a few years earlier for my private place to write. But the inspiration was slow in coming. Many ideas flew around in my brain, but I couldn't think how to put them into a pattern. And our afternoons were filled with responding to calls from our fruit trees. We were still farmers. Apples and prune plums ripened and clamored to be picked and processed.

Herb's style of writing often took the form of being swept up by a wide, imaginative vision that led him to pour out several pages of free-flowing language in a short time. So I was not surprised, when I came in at noon one day, to hear him say, "I've had a great idea for the dialogue!"

There was no stopping him, so I reconciled myself to postponing lunch until he read me his sample pages.

I never knew what to expect when he came forth with his strong enthusiasms, like for a new play. I was unsure whether his passion was truly moved by the Spirit, or whether he was being carried away by something unworthy or unworkable. I would ask myself, "Is he an ego-maniac or a genius?"

He had spoken of our being strangers to each other, for we were always changing and growing. He was a stranger, a beloved stranger, one whose personality constantly unfolded in new ways. Maybe he *was* a genius.

But on this particular day, as he read his sample pages aloud, my heart sank. It seemed to me that his writing was full of arrogance and didactic formulas. No way could I see myself participating in a skit of that kind.

"I'm sorry, Herb," I said, "I just don't like what you've written at all!"

He looked deflated. He tried to convince me, but I stood my ground.

At last he said, "Well, you go finish writing your version, and then I'll look at it."

I wrote what I could, but, as always, it took longer for me than for him. And other things kept intruding into my time: grocery shopping, dentist appointments, social events, figs and grapes ready for picking.

Ten days before October 15, I still hadn't completed my sample. I awoke feeling tired and vaguely depressed. Herb made some kind of comment he intended as a joke, but in my vulnerable mood it reduced me to tears.

"Hey, what's the matter?" he asked.

"Oh, I don't know," I blubbered. "I'm tired. And I guess I'm anxious over too many things to do. Especially that dialogue."

Herb showed instant sympathy. "I'm tired too," he admitted. "And I'm realizing we've got to cut some things out." He stroked my thigh. "Maybe we can't go to that wedding in Sacramento on Saturday."

The pressure eased as we agreed to cancel some of our commitments. "After all," we told each other, "we're retired. We don't have to do anything!"

We set a time to confront, together, the requirement of the dialogue. With clipboards and pencils, we sat down in the study, Herb behind his desk and I in a chair across from him.

"Let's not think of this as a duty," Herb suggested. "It's an opportunity, isn't it? To give creative expression to what our experience together has been? And, like so many other things in our life, let's both work on it."

I felt cheered already. As we began brainstorming, we sparked each other off, tossing ideas back and forth.

"I'd like to see us give an example of how we learned to accept each other's ways of doing things," I said. "Like, when I washed a big mess of dishes, how it irritated me to have you pile them up higher and higher in the dish rack, when the obvious and efficient way would be to put some of them in our second rack. Then one day you told me you were using the dishes and pans to build a piece of architecture. I saw that it was a game, a recreation for you, and on that basis I could accept it."

Herb was making notes. "Yes, let's put that in. And let's tell how I dominated you in not letting you get your hair cut."

Images came thick and fast. Part of every day we devoted to pouring them out, selecting, and gradually herding them into some kind of order. By the end of the week we had put together a little drama that satisfied both of us reasonably well. And by the afternoon of Friday the thirteenth, Herb had put our fifteen-minute offering on the computer and printed a copy for each of us. Our biggest labor was ended.

That evening, as we stood in the kitchen facing each other after finishing the dishes, I was overcome with a surge of love for my dearest.

"Let's jump for joy," I said, proposing a ritual we'd observed a number of times before.

We grasped hands and literally jumped an inch or two off the floor. Then we fell into each other's arms laughing.

The date of our Golden Wedding, or, as we had come to speak of it, the celebrating of our entire "Golden Marriage," fell on Sunday, just as it had fifty years ago in Berkeley. The affair was to run from two to six.

Since Gil and his helpers would manage all the last-minute details, Herb and I spent a quiet Sabbath morning. He polished his Birkenstock sandals, and I cleaned my white purse. After clearing up from an early lunch, all we had to do was wait for Gil, who had insisted that he would chauffeur us in his own car.

Decked out in our finery, we sat in the living room in comfortable, upholstered arm chairs. I was wearing a silky, ruffled white dress I'd picked up in a consignment shop for twelve dollars. Herb was resplendent in the brown velvet pants and velvet paisley jacket he had bought on sale several years before and only wore on very special occasions.

"I like the way your white necktie matches your snow-white hair," I said. My sense of humor bubbled up into a smile. "When I first married you, it never occurred to me that some day your hair would be white."

"You never know what you're getting into when you get married, do you?" Herb mused as he leaned against the chair back. "Not only white hair. The problems and gropings, and the joys."

"What we 'got into' has made our life so rich," I said dreamily. "Rich beyond my wildest dreams."

"Mine too. And it gets better all the time," Herb added with conviction.

We heard Gil's car on our gravel driveway, and soon we were ensconced in its back seat. As he drove us up the winding road to Grass Valley, Gil kept up a pleasant chatter, and Herb's occasional responses kept it from being a monologue.

But I was absorbed in my own thoughts. I remembered the prophetic comments my father had made at our wedding in 1939 about marriage as an "Unfinished Symphony." Our personal symphony did not stop at fifty years. It was still unfinished, and would always be so. And it was more than just the social institution, "marriage." For us, the experience of living together through thick and thin, getting to know one person so deeply, had helped us relate more lovingly to other persons. Perhaps one day, I mused, we could see and value everyone in the world with as much understanding and compassion as we felt for each other.

Gil let us out in front of the performing arts center and went to park his car. Hand in hand, Herb and I mounted the few steps. We exchanged fond glances. Then Herb reached out to the shiny knob, and opened the door.